The Death of Peter Pan

THE DEATH OF PETER PAN was first published as a paperback and eBook in 2014 by Lydian Press.

The Death of Peter Pan © 1989, 2014 Barry Lowe
ISBN 978-1-909934-45-0

Barry Lowe is hereby identified as the author of this play in accordance with section 77 of the Copyright, Designs and Patents Act 1988. The author has asserted his moral rights.

Cover Design: Dawné Dominique

The Death of Peter Pan

Barry Lowe

 Playscript

BARRY LOWE

www.barrylowe.info
www.facebook.com/barry.lowe.3591

Born in Sydney, Australia, he has worked as a journalist and fiction writer. His theatrical career began as lighting operator for a children's theatre group and his first produced plays were for children. His first produced adult play was *Writer's Cramp* (Gay Theatre Company), after which he spent the next few years writing a new play every six weeks ('my repertory years' he calls them) and works included *Ego Positioning, Lyrics for a Lost Love Song, The Finishing School, Elbow Grease, The Extraordinary Annual General Meeting of the Size-Queen Club, Lip Service, Sal, Rosaleen: Wicked Witch of the Cross,* and *Lettuce Cutlets.*

Later works, produced in Australia as well as the UK, North America, and Italy, include *Seeing Things, Heir Raising, The Barricade, Tokyo Rose, Dutch Courage* (songs by Sean Peter), *Scam!* (also with Sean Peter), *She's No Angel: A Mae West Vaudeville* (with Sean Peter), *The Death of Peter Pan, Homme Fatale: The Joey Stefano Story, By the Short & Curlies, A Thousand and One Night Stands: The Life of Jon Vincent,* and *Relative Merits* (Australian Writers Guild Award short listed). He has also adapted *The Great Gatsby* and *The Turn of the Screw* for stage and adapted *Oscar Wilde's The Importance of Being Earnest (as performed by the inmates at Reading Gaol).*

He is the author of *Atomic Blonde: The Life and Films of Mamie Van Doren* (McFarland).

CAST OF CHARACTERS

JAMES BARRIE *Scottish playwright and author, about 60*

MICHAEL LLEWELYN DAVIES *One of Barrie's adopted sons, late teens/early twenties*

ROGER SENHOUSE *Friend of Michael's, late teens/early twenties*

RUPERT BUXTON *Late teens/early twenties*

ARTHUR BASSETT *Fellow student of Michael's, late teens/early twenties*

MARY ANSELL *Former wife of James Barrie.*

'NICO' LLEWELYN DAVIES: *Michael's younger brother, mid-to-late teens.*

NURSE

FRENCH WAITER

FRENCH PROSTITUTE

HOUSEMASTER (Voice)

Setting

THE DEATH OF PETER PAN *is set in the last two years of the life of Michael Llewelyn Davies, late 1918 to early 1921, and takes place in James Barrie's London house, at Eton, a French cafe, a Paris pensione, the banks of the River Seine, the Scottish island of Eilean Shona, Oxford, and the recesses of the character's minds.*

"Hope" **by Rupert Buxton used by kind permission of Kate Bowles.**

THE DEATH OF PETER PAN was first produced at La Mama, Carlton, by Performing Arts Projects, on 16 August, 1989, with the following cast:

JAMES MATTHEW BARRIE	**John Paisley**
MICHAEL LLEWELYN DAVIES	**David Tredinnick**
RUPERT BUXTON	**Sam Sejavka**
ARTHUR BASSETT	**Timothy Jones**
ROGER SENHOUSE	**Kevin Hopkins**
'NICO' LLEWELYN DAVIES	**Matthew McConnon**
MARY ANSELL	**Fiona Ferguson**
FRENCH PROSTITUTE	**Andrea Swifte**
FRENCH WAITER	**Patrick Le Conte**

Director	Robert Chuter
Set Designer	Marc Raszewski
Costume Designer	Neville Kerr
Stage Manager	Belinda Davis
Lighting Designer & Operator	Christopher Coe
Sound Designer	Donald Baldie
ASM/Sound Operator	Monika Arnold
Assistant to the Director	Anna Schlusser
Photographer	Marc Phee

The production was revived, with minor changes, at the Universal 2, Fitzroy, opening on 26 October, 1989, with Richard Aspel as Arthur Bassett, and Fiona Ferguson as the French Prostitute, with Lighting Design by Stephen Kainey, and Christina Pedder & Anna Schlusser as Production Assistants.

A revised version of THE DEATH OF PETER PAN was first presented in Sydney at the New Theatre, in association with the Sydney Gay & Lesbian Mardi Gras, opening on 17 February, 1995, with the following cast:

JAMES MATTHEW BARRIE	**Barry Latchford**
MICHAEL LLEWELYN DAVIES	**John Galagher**
RUPERT BUXTON	**David Owens**
ROGER SENHOUSE	**Simon Stollery**
ARTHUR BASSETT	**Stuart Katzen**
'NICO' LLEWELYN DAVIES	**Matt Jenkins**
MARY ANSELL	**Wendy Hill**
HOUSEMASTER/WAITER	**John Grinston**
PROSTITUTE/NURSE	**Janet Gibson** alternating with **Tasma Walton**

Director	Elaine Hudson
Set/Costume/Poster Designer	John King
Lighting Designer	Tony Youlden
Original Music	Betty Leonie
Production Manager	Joanne Duffy
Stage Manager	Monica Furnan
Assistant Stage Manager	Sally Freeman
Lighting Operators	Kylie Mascord & Mark Fordham
Sound Operator	Nhan Chiem
Dance Routines	Gill Falson
Set Construction Supervisor	Tom Bannerman

For Walter Figallo, who is always there

Special thanks to Robert Chuter, Elaine Hudson, Natalie Mosco, Lester Shane, and the various casts and crews who have helped refine and bring this play to life in readings and productions across the world.

Act One

Scene 1

Lights up on JAMES BARRIE *wrapped in a blanket. He is smoking a pipe and coughing badly. Every time he takes a puff of his pipe he attempts to brush the smoke away with his hand. He has a Scottish accent.*

BARRIE: *(to audience)* It's a pity about sons. By the time they reach six or seven they're too old to jiggle on your knee. And by the time they reach twelve or thirteen, giving you just enough time to pluck up the courage to tell then you love them, they've become embarrassed by emotion, so you keep it to yourself and sometimes it never gets said. Sons. I had five of them. George, Jack, Peter, Michael and Nicholas. Though we never called him Nicholas. Always Nico. Not that they were my children exactly. Well, I wasn't their real father. Although they wanted for nothing in my care. I gave them more than their real parents, Sylvia and Arthur, could ever have dreamed of. Especially George and Michael. They were my favourites. But George, he was killed in action during The Great War. In France. Where he's buried. In fact, I was visiting his grave site when peace was declared. And Michael… My own lost boy.

He is becoming emotional and takes a puff of his pipe to calm his nerves which precipitates a coughing fit he cannot stop. He attempts to hide his pipe as nurse enters.

NURSE: Sir James, I've told you about getting yourself excited. Now, why aren't you in bed? You should be resting from your nasty flu.

BARRIE: The most contemptible thing about the flu is its damnably inadequate name.

NURSE: I'm sure it's a perfectly good name for it.

BARRIE: I think I shall try Christian Science. There can be nothing more exasperating to a good sharp pain than insisting blandly that it isn't there.

Nurse discovers his pipe.

NURSE: And you'll never get better if you continue to smoke this nasty thing.

BARRIE: Don't treat me like an obstreperous child.

NURSE: If that's how you behave then that's how you will be treated. No more smoking! Your lungs simply aren't up to it.

Barrie produces a water bottle from his bed.

BARRIE: What in heaven's name is this?

NURSE: It's your hot water bottle. Part of the treatment to get you better.

Barrie finds another hot water bottle in his bed.

BARRIE: There are as many hot water bottles in my bed as there are runs on an Australian cricket team's Test score sheet.

The nurse replaces the hot water bottles in his bed.

NURSE: All I know is hot water bottles will do you good.

BARRIE: Even if I drink them they won't help this cough and I must have some sleep. *(coughs)* It's enough to wrench the heart out of me.

His cough gets progressively worse and the nurse taps his chest.

Would you kindly refrain from tapping away at my chest as if it were a front door.

Coughs again.

NURSE: You're putting that on.

BARRIE: Then I shall lie here and sulk with just my cough for company.

Coughs.

NURSE: Stop it this instant! You are such an exasperating patient.

The Nurse collects his medication from a bureau in his rooms. Barrie watches her.

BARRIE: Heroin. A sedative for my throat and my lungs. As well as my mind. It lays to rest the ghosts.

NURSE: You must promise you will try to get some rest, Sir James. Promise me.

BARRIE: I promise.

The Nurse administers the heroin.

NURSE: There now. You'll feel a lot better in a few minutes. I'll be right next door and I'll look in on you from time to time. Just relax or you'll never get well.

She exits.

BARRIE: *(addresses the audience)* I miss them, my poor dead boys. I should like to see them one more time but I know that no one should come back no matter how much he is loved. But I did dream that Michael came back to me. I dreamed we had an extra year together and during that time we lived quite ordinarily though strangely close to each other. I did some things that I had wanted to do before but until then had not dared do. I had fears of spoiling him and struggled not to do it. In agony I let him go away sometimes, to live the ordinary life of youth.

The sound of fireworks and merriment. Eton. Armistice night: November, 1918. BASSETT, SENHOUSE and MICHAEL LLEWELYN DAVIES stagger on slightly drunk, banging tin bath tubs. Other sounds of celebration off.

BASSETT: Righto, Davies, down on your knees and thank your own particular gods the war is over just one day before your call-up.

SENHOUSE: I don't really think James Barrie had anything to do with it, Bassett.

MICHAEL: I should not be a bit surprised if old Uncle Jim did have something to do with ending the war.

BASSETT: Confound his interference! And just as we were winning, too.

They all laugh.

SENHOUSE: And where is the gentleman who is the topic of our conversation?

MICHAEL: In Paris. In the thick of it.

BASSETT: Heaven help our fighting men.

SENHOUSE: You can be a frightful bounder sometimes, Bassett.

MICHAEL: He set up a hospital and nursing home in memory of my brother George.

BASSETT: I say, Davies, I am awfully sorry. I was only teasing.

Sound of fireworks.

MICHAEL: Let's go and watch the fireworks.

BASSETT: You know what the Housemaster said about being back in our rooms by curfew.

SENHOUSE: Don't be such a wet blanket, Bassett. Nobody is taking any notice of the rules tonight. I'll wager even the Housemaster himself will be at the fireworks. I'm game if you are, Davies.

MICHAEL: I'm game. What about you, Bassett?

BASSETT: Oh, all right. But we mustn't be too late back.

They whoop and rush about. Michael accidentally bumps into a stranger who has appeared. RUPERT BUXTON is dressed as an aesthete. Michael has run into Buxton but it is Buxton who apologises.

BUXTON: I do beg your pardon, that was most careless of me.

He smiles and moves on as Michael and the others glare at him.

BASSETT: Did you see the way he dresses?

SENHOUSE: And that hair!

BASSETT: I should like to give the scoundrel a good thrashing. He brings Eton into disrepute.

Buxton turns to address them.

BUXTON: Ah, but I do not attend Eton, my good sirs. I come from Harrow.

SENHOUSE: Come on, Davies. We'll miss the best part of the fireworks.

MICHAEL: You go ahead. I'll be along presently.

SENHOUSE: Don't get into an argument.

Bassett and Senhouse exit. Michael continues to stare.

BUXTON: Why do you stare with such contempt? After all, God made me too.

MICHAEL: Then He is getting careless.

BUXTON: (*laughing*) I see. And on the eighth day God created Eton.

MICHAEL: You have no right to be on these grounds.

BUXTON: Ah! The unwritten eleventh commandment of all British Public School Boys. Thou shalt not visit Eton if you are a Harrow Man.

MICHAEL: Have you no respect?

BUXTON: For whom? For myself? Yes. For God? I don't believe in him.

MICHAEL: You're an atheist!

BUXTON: It's all the rage at Harrow.

Despite himself, Michael is intrigued by Buxton.

MICHAEL: I wouldn't dare.

BUXTON: Then there's the difference between us. I do. Do I know you?

MICHAEL: No. But I wish you did.

BUXTON: I say. Let us pretend I do.

Buxton takes Michael's arm before they move off.

Come along then.

MICHAEL: The fireworks and my friends are that way.

BUXTON: I have no use for anything as mundane as fireworks. Nor for your friends from what I saw of them.

Michael hesitates.

Make up your mind then. An evening of excruciating banality with your friends and your fireworks or an evening of unbridled interest with me.

MICHAEL: Where shall we go?

BUXTON: First we shall find an innkeeper who will exchange a bottle of his finest liquor for this dowdy coat of mine and then we shall drink ourselves into friendship. And if I still like you at the end of the evening then we shall be great chums indeed.

MICHAEL: There is no need to dispose of your coat. I have a little money.

BUXTON: Never have just a little money. Always have none or a great deal. Anything in between is bourgeois. Safe.

MICHAEL: Boring.

BUXTON: Exactly!

MICHAEL: And what brings you to Eton? It must be frightfully important.

BUXTON: Of the utmost seriousness. I have heard that an academic gentleman from this hallowed institution has said in public that the life and works of James Matthew Barrie have an immoral tendency.

MICHAEL: My Uncle Jim? Immoral tendencies?

BUXTON: I had heard rumors that one of his sons attended Eton.

MICHAEL: Michael Llewelyn Davies at your service.

BUXTON: How extraordinarily fortunate to have run into you like this.

MICHAEL: Uncle Jim is extremely possessive of his good standing. He says it's a comfort to him like warm milk and a sugary biscuit before bed.

BUXTON: Then the cad who made the accusation must be found out and forced to apologise. This is my quest. Will you join me on it?

MICHAEL: I'll be Sancho Panza to your Don Quixote. And try to keep you out of trouble.

Scene 2

Later that night. Michael and Buxton, minus his coat, enter. They are drunk and staggering. Buxton is singing and Michael is attempting to get him to keep quiet.

MICHAEL: Shh! You'll wake the entire school. And the Housemaster. Then I shall be for it.

BUXTON: No sir! The cad who shall be for it is he who has sullied the spotless reputation of James Barrie.

MICHAEL: I sometimes think heretically that it's a character that might improve with a little judicious smudging.

BUXTON: *(shouting)* Come out, you scoundrel, and show your face. Where is the cad who dares blacken the name of

Scotland's greatest writer? (*quieter*) Come on, Davies, don't be a slacker.

MICHAEL: We'll wake the Housemaster.

BUXTON: You're not afraid, are you? Of the Housemaster? Of a few whacks of the ruddy cane?

MICHAEL: Of course not.

BUXTON: Then help me weed out the human excrement who dares call James Barrie unwholesome.

MICHAEL: And what should we do if he does appear?

BUXTON: We shall roast him for Sunday lunch!

MICHAEL: (*giggling*) I say, what a splendid idea. (*shouting*) Come out you coward!

> *Buxton yells too but they are out of sync.*

BUXTON: Here, that's no use. Let's try it together. Much more forceful. After three. One. Two. Three.

MICHAEL/BUXTON: Shame on Eton for harboring a scoundrel who dares blacken the name of Scotland's greatest dramatist.

> *Buxton slips away.*

Show your face at once or face the consequences.

> *Bassett and Senhouse stagger on.*

SENHOUSE: What's all the noise?

BASSETT: Where did you get to, Davies? We waited an age for you to show up.

MICHAEL: I've been having the most wonderful time with... whatsisname here...

BASSETT: You're drunk!

SENHOUSE: Let he who is without sin and so forth.

BASSETT: Don't quote homilies at me, Senhouse.

MICHAEL: Where did he go? He was here a minute ago.

SENHOUSE: Who?

MICHAEL: That chap we passed earlier in the evening.

BASSETT: The one from Harrow?

MICHAEL: That's him! (*calling*) Where are you, Mr Harrow Man? Come out, come out, wherever you are!

SENHOUSE: For heaven's sake, be quiet.

MICHAEL: Come out, come out, wherever you are. I know you're hiding.

A light goes on and there is the sound of a window opening.

HOUSEMASTER: (*voice off*) Who is making all that noise?

Senhouse and Bassett have the presence of mind to scatter. not so Michael.

MICHAEL: (*still trying to find Buxton*) I know you're here. Somewhere.

HOUSEMASTER: (*off*) Is that you, Davies?

MICHAEL: I've lost someone ...

HOUSEMASTER: (*off*) What do you think you're doing?

MICHAEL: I'm looking for him, sir.

HOUSEMASTER: (*off*) You're drunk! How dare you come in at this times of night.

MICHAEL: But it's a glorious night. Armistice. I shan't have to go into the army after all.

HOUSEMASTER: (*off*) I can understand a few good natured high jinks on such a night, but to wake the entire school...

BASSETT: (*whispering*) For God's sake shut up, Davies. You'll just make it worse.

HOUSEMASTER: (*off*) Who else is out there?

MICHAEL: No one, sir.

HOUSEMASTER: (*off*) Come on, I heard voices. Own up or I shall come down and drag you out of hiding by the scruff of your neck.

Senhouse and Bassett appear sheepishly.

HOUSEMASTER: (*off*) Senhouse and Bassett. I should have known. The Three Musketeers. Very well. I assume you have secret ways of getting back into your rooms for I shall not open the doors. And I expect to see you all in my study tomorrow morning at nine o'clock. Sharp. Be on time, gentlemen. Good night.

Sound of window closing. The three students stare at one another for a moment before bursting into laughter.

Scene 3

Michael and James Barrie are walking through the grounds of Eton

BARRIE: I think the Housemaster remarkably lenient under the circumstances. Five hundred lines and a detention. You got off rather lightly. If I had been Housemaster, why you'd be in detention still.

MICHAEL: You're not too angry, Uncle Jim?

BARRIE: A harmless prank. A noisy one admittedly. But I doubt many people slept that night.

MICHAEL: And was it awfully bad? In France, I mean.

BARRIE: Paris was all lit up and there were cries everywhere of 'It's finished! It's finished!' And I saw German prisoners being brought in who didn't know about the Armistice. They had been dug out of the ground.

MICHAEL: It all sounds so jolly. I'm sorry now to have missed it.

BARRIE: *(he doesn't want to make it sound too romantic)* In the country it was very different. The villages are in dreadful condition, some of them have one house standing in fifty. On the Marne I saw an old woman knitting placidly by the door of her new wooden house. On the same spot she had been *(choosing the word carefully)* ill-treated by two German soldiers in their dash for Paris and they destroyed her original home. Now, on their dash back to Germany, they lie buried beneath her potatoes and she sits there knitting. And there are thousands of them buried in the surrounding countryside. A grim notice has been issued to chain up the dogs at night. They had taken to wandering. And digging.

MICHAEL: *(shuddering)* Brother George?

BARRIE: They say he is buried near Ypres, where there was so much fighting. I know that ground very well now.

MICHAEL: Were you in terrible danger when you went there?

BARRIE: No, the day was quite belching with sunshine. Not the kind of day to let one stay out of sorts for long. Even when a favourite son lies buried beneath the soil. There were primroses there and they gave me enormous pleasure. The courage of flowers in those days to go on just as usual.

MICHAEL: Was George your favourite, Uncle Jim?

BARRIE: One shouldn't have a favourite, I suppose, but if I did, if, mind you, yes, it would have been George.

MICHAEL: Now I shall be your favourite, Uncle Jim. Shall I?

BARRIE: Would you like to be?

MICHAEL: Yes, please.

BARRIE: It would mean being good to your old Uncle Jim.

MICHAEL: But I am already. I write to you every day. What else must I do?

BARRIE: *(sighs)* Indeed, what else is there?

MICHAEL: *(sensing Barrie is about to go into one of his moods)* What did you bring me from Paris? Did you bring me a present?

BARRIE: A chocolate cake.

MICHAEL: My favourite! I shall be the envy of Eton. Just one cake, Uncle Jim?

BARRIE: You are so inordinately fond of puddings that you cannot enjoy the first helping for thinking of the second.

MICHAEL: I shall plant little flags in it of all the valiant, victorious nations.

BARRIE: You are still so young.

MICHAEL: Not so very, Uncle Jim.

BARRIE: *(something they have talked about before)* And have you decided?

MICHAEL: I should very much like to go around the world. Would you mind dreadfully?

BARRIE: Not dreadfully.

MICHAEL: But you would mind?

BARRIE: I think I should mind a little.

MICHAEL: Let me see then. My second choice.

BARRIE: Oxford?

MICHAEL: Oh, Uncle Jim. I don't want to go to Oxford and learn solemn things. That's your choice, not mine.

BARRIE: Then what is the young man's choice?

MICHAEL: *(wary)* I should like to...

BARRIE: Tell me.

MICHAEL: I should like to run away to Paris.

BARRIE: What would you do in Paris?

MICHAEL: Live in an artist's garret. Paint.

BARRIE: And Oxford?

MICHAEL: Damn Oxford! I shall hate it there. Just like I did Eton. I say, what about letting me go to the Sorbonne. I speak fluent French and that way I can set up my easel on the Left Bank, and wear a beret and become an artist.

BARRIE: I don't think the mere wearing of a beret qualifies one as an artist.

MICHAEL: Paris is not so dreadfully far.

BARRIE: But my first choice is Oxford.

MICHAEL: And it's my last choice.

BARRIE: *(changing the subject to avoid an argument)* Tell me more about your young friend and his gallant defence of my reputation.

MICHAEL: He was extraordinary. And to think I insulted him at first.

BARRIE: Sometimes our greatest friendships begin with insults.

MICHAEL: We talked and talked.

BARRIE: And had more than a little to drink.

MICHAEL: Fortifying ourselves against the scoundrel who insulted your standing.

BARRIE: I would like to meet this extraordinary young man and thank him personally for his interjection in the assault on my position.

MICHAEL: But that's just it! I forgot to ask his name. Or he was never forthcoming. I don't quite remember which.

BARRIE: Should you manage to trace him bring him up to town for a visit.

MICHAEL: I shall ask at Harrow. He must be well known for he dresses so peculiarly.

BARRIE: And you will think about Oxford?

MICHAEL: Paris!

BARRIE: *(firmly)* Being a favourite does entail some responsibility.

MICHAEL: Uncle Jim, I'll play you at billiards. And if I win, it's Paris.

BARRIE: And if I win?

MICHAEL: We'll talk some more about Oxford.

Scene 4

James Barrie addresses the audience.

BARRIE: So, you have gone to Paris which seems all the farther away from me because I never dare attempt to pronounce the names of its suburbs to one who speaks French so fluently. It's like an extra barrier, an additional intimation that you have burned your boats, a reminder that you are of those who don't do things by halves. And your letters are full of accusative commas and semi-colons. Or else, unaccustomary silences. You have had your revenge. Be forgiving. If Oxford is such anathema to you then I bow to your wishes. But please, no more silences. They are unbearable.

Scene 5

Paris, 1919. Michael, Senhouse and Bassett.

SENHOUSE: Who would have expected so many people to be here? It's choc-a-bloc.

BASSETT: They're all here for that tedious peace procession.

MICHAEL: Tedious? I thought it was grand.

BASSETT: I'm tired and hungry.

SENHOUSE: Your trouble, Bassett, is you don't have an adventurous soul.

BASSETT: Adventure, Senhouse, is not sitting up a tree all night on the Champs Elysees waiting for a lot of soldiers to parade by.

MICHAEL: But Paris is the city of romance.

BASSETT: Not when it looks as if we'll have to spend another night in that self-same tree.

SENHOUSE: So where do we sleep tonight?

MICHAEL: By the Seine. Can you think of anything more intoxicating?

BASSETT: The smell of the prison cell after the agents de police arrest us.

MICHAEL: If money can't buy us lodgings let's at least fill our stomachs. What about here? This looks a nice cafe?

They seat themselves at an outdoor café. Bassett blanches at the prices.

BASSETT: Steady on, Davies. This place is a bit rich for my appetite.

SENHOUSE: Don't be such a bore, Bassett.

MICHAEL: Not enough pocket money from papa?

BASSETT: That's unfair, Davies. Your Uncle Jim picks up the tab for you.

SENHOUSE: Though you've not been a conscientious correspondent on this trip, Davies. Won't he be peeved?

MICHAEL: Of course, but this is his little gift for my successfully completing Eton. And he will pay for both of you as well. It will be his way of apologising to his favourite son for pushing Oxford at him. Of course, his little scheme is to get me so thoroughly debauched with Paris that I'll come galloping back.

SENHOUSE: This place is awfully expensive.

MICHAEL: I don't think he'll begrudge it. Not if I do decide to go to Oxford after all. Though I dread the thought of it.

BASSETT: Oh, do think about it, Davies. Senhouse and I will be quite lost without you at Oxford.

Senhouse is flirting with the Waiter.

Won't we, Senhouse? Senhouse!

SENHOUSE: Ah, quite. Quite lost.

Waiter comes to the table.

WAITER: Bonjour messieurs.

MICHAEL: Bonjour.

SENHOUSE: Hello.

Bassett grunts.

SENHOUSE: Paris has definitely just become more interesting.

BASSETT: Senhouse!

WAITER: Qu'est-ce que vous prenez, messieurs?

MICHAEL: Du thé et du gâteau, s'il vous plaît. Oh, vous avez du gâteau chocolat?

WAITER: Bien sûr. On est à Paris, ici.

MICHAEL: Alors du thé et du gâteau chocolat.

WAITER: Bien, monsieur.

SENHOUSE: Ruddy chocolate gâteau again.

BASSETT: Davies, when I said I was hungry I expected something a little more substantial than chocolate cake. Don't you ever get sick of it?

MICHAEL: I'd live on it if I could.

SENHOUSE: Oxford will be such fun, Davies. It won't be at all like Eton. There will be lots of new friends.

MICHAEL: For you perhaps.

BASSETT: And for you if you stop being so dour and impenetrable.

MICHAEL: I have to be careful with whom I mix publicly.

SENHOUSE: *(good naturedly)* Snotty-nosed little swat.

BASSETT: Some of those friends of yours, Senhouse, are so obvious. Take Marjoribanks, for example...

SENHOUSE: His obviousness is what makes him such fun.

MICHAEL: And I like Marjoribanks.

Waiter comes back.

SENHOUSE: And I like Paris.

WAITER: The best chocolat gâteau in all of France for the visiting English gentlemen.

MICHAEL: You speak English?

WAITER: But not as well as the young gentleman speaks French. You are enjoying your visit, non?

MICHAEL: Magnificent city. Paris.

BASSETT: What we've seen of it.

WAITER: But you must see it all.

SENHOUSE: Yes, we'd like that.

BASSETT: Senhouse!

WAITER: *(laughs)* It is all right, monsieur. We French have none of your English...er

Tries a few French expressions.

MICHAEL: *(helpfully)* Reserve.

WAITER: Yes, that is the correct word. Reserve.

SENHOUSE: That is refreshing. *(flirting)* Where do you recommend we begin?

WAITER: I have a few suggestions for the beau monsieur.

SENHOUSE: Suggest away!

WAITER: *(looking specifically at Senhouse)* But, if you wish, I would be happy to show you around la belle Paris.

BASSETT: No thank you.

WAITER: Pardonnez-moi until I have served these other customers. Bon Appetit.

Waiter exits.

BASSETT: For heaven's sake, Senhouse. You made such a spectacle of yourself.

SENHOUSE: *(watching the Waiter's every move)* Do you think we shall fall terribly in love at Oxford?

MICHAEL: It will just get in the way of study if you do.

SENHOUSE: And you accuse me of having no romance in my soul.

MICHAEL: Everything in its proper time and place.

SENHOUSE: *(still watching the Waiter)* Love is so unpredictable.

BASSETT: *(seriously)* And the consummating of it so messy.

MICHAEL: Well, I shan't go running out to look for it.

SENHOUSE: *(deliberately needling Michael)* To fall in love, really in love, would be an awfully big adventure.

Michael playfully throws cake at Senhouse.

MICHAEL: Don't quote that play at me. You know I hate it.

Senhouse throws cake back at him.

SENHOUSE: Do you really? It made you what you are today.

Senhouse and Michael continue to throw cake at each other until they realise Bassett is not joining in the fun. They then turn their attention to him until it becomes a three-way battle. After a moment Michael stops while the other two continue. Michael has just seen Buxton enter.

SENHOUSE: What is it, Davies? Are you all right, old chap?

Bassett sees Buxton.

BASSETT: It's him!

SENHOUSE: It's who?

BASSETT: You know! The frightful chap from Harrow! The night of the fireworks.

MICHAEL: I want to invite him over but I don't know his name.

BASSETT: What?!?

SENHOUSE: After the way he ran away leaving you to carry the blame for his bad behaviour.

BASSETT: The man's a fraud. I don't like him one bit.

MICHAEL: Invite him to join us one of you.

BASSETT: Why should we?

SENHOUSE: We don't even know him.

MICHAEL: Please, Senhouse. For me.

SENHOUSE: Very well, Davies. But I protest if this fellow is going to ruin our holiday.

Senhouse goes to Buxton and points out the table where they are sitting. Buxton's face lights up in recognition and he comes over.

BUXTON: This is rather unexpected seeing you again, especially like this, Davies. Quite a magnificent city, Paris. Don't you agree?

BASSETT: You know you got us into the most frightful bother last year!

MICHAEL: Bassett!

BASSETT: Well he did!

BUXTON: Sorry about that, chaps, but I had to catch my train.

SENHOUSE: We had no name to blame it on.

BUXTON: Awfully rude of me, I know. Buxton. Rupert.

SENHOUSE: Senhouse. Roger.

BASSETT: *(grumbling)* Bassett. Arthur Bassett.

BUXTON: And you, of course, are still Davies. Michael Llewelyn.

MICHAEL: At your service.

BUXTON: I am awfully sorry about that last time we met.

MICHAEL: Won't you join us? Please?

Buxton scrapes cake from Michael's face.

BUXTON: Looks as if I'd be intruding.

MICHAEL: *(embarrassed)* Just a silly prank.

Michael hands Buxton a serviette to wipe the cake from his fingers but instead Buxton licks his fingers clean before he wipes them.

SENHOUSE: Celebrating our acceptance at Oxford.

BUXTON: Great news, indeed! And great news I share with you.

BASSETT: *(disgusted)* What!

SENHOUSE: You, too?

BUXTON: Yes.

SENHOUSE: Splendid! Do sit down and join us, won't you?

Bassett glares.

BUXTON: Thanks, but I can't at present. I must push on. Have some business to attend to. But, I say, where are you chaps staying? Perhaps, later...

SENHOUSE: Our present address is up a tree on the Champs Elysees.

BUXTON: Mm, accommodation is scarce. There's an idea. Help to make up for my behavior. You're all quite welcome to share my digs.

SENHOUSE: Why, thank you, Buxton. That's most sporting of you.

BUXTON: Bit unsavory, but it's a place to sleep all the same.

BASSETT: What exactly do you mean by 'unsavory'?

BUXTON: It's rather small. In fact, it only comfortably sleeps two. No, I exaggerate. It only takes two uncomfortably. It's in Montmartre.

BASSETT: Oh, God.

BUXTON: It's usually rented by the hour but I managed to bribe the concierge to let me have it for a few days. More money than she makes from the ladies of the night. But, if you do decide to make use of it you'll have to take it in turns. Two at a time. I shan't be back until late. *(takes out a key)* Here's the key. *(writes the address on a napkin and hands it to Michael)* There's the address. But whoever decides to share with me will have to wait up to let me in.

MICHAEL: *(quickly)* I'll wait up for you, Buxton.

BUXTON: Then bonsoir until later.

Buxton picks up Michael's cup of tea and drains it.

And, say, Davies, I hear you're good at cricket. Perhaps you might like to bowl a few overs with me some time.

He exits.

BASSETT: The more heartily we drink the sooner we reach the dregs.

MICHAEL: What an unusual fellow.

BASSETT: I don't much fancy sharing a bed with Senhouse.

SENHOUSE: Any more than I fancy sharing it with you, Bassett. *(looking toward the Waiter)* But then, you might not have to.

BASSETT: But better by far than sharing it with that Buxton chap.

SENHOUSE: *(winking at Michael)* At least you can talk about cricket, eh, Davies?

Michael begins the cake fight again at the innuendo.

BASSETT: Won't you two ever grow up?

The Waiter enters and sees the mess. He swears vehemently in French.

Scene 6

Bassett addresses the audience.

BASSETT: Michael Llewelyn Davies was one of the most remarkable people I ever met, very sensitive and emotional, but he concealed both to a large extent. He had a profound influence on virtually everyone who became his friend - particularly Roger Senhouse. At Eton they forged one of those intense special emotional friendships, although they had the good manners to keep it discreet. And non-physical. I knew it to be merely a phase they were going through and would grow out of soon enough. But I didn't like the influence Buxton had on Davies. Buxton was exceptionally clever, with a real lust for life. He was dark and there were shadowy depths to him that I thought he would pull Davies down into. He thumbed his nose at established convention. I remember Davies once asked me...

MICHAEL: Why don't you like my being friends with Rupert Buxton?

BASSETT: 'I have a feeling of doom about him,' I said. But my friendship with Davies and, yes, even Senhouse, although his increasing obviousness got on my nerves, was perfection. Those Eton days were the happiest of my life. We were The Three Musketeers, but when Buxton came along, the camaraderie was broken.

Scene 7

Buxton's lodgings. Michael is waiting at the lift of the pensione for Buxton's return. He is cradling a bottle of red wine and a French bread stick. Buxton enters in high spirits.

BUXTON: I say, Davies, you are a stick waiting up for me like this.

MICHAEL: I thought you might be hungry.

BUXTON: Ravenous. I have such an appetite.

He is about to tear into the bread but gets an idea.

Have you ever swum in the Seine as the sun rises?

MICHAEL: I don't swim.

BUXTON: Then I shall teach you. Come on then...

MICHAEL: I don't like the water. Not over my head at any rate.

BUXTON: Then we shall have a marvellous breakfast beside one of the world's most romantic rivers.

MICHAEL: What about Senhouse and Bassett?

BUXTON: This morning, Davies, it shall be just you and me. We will open our beings to Paris and allow it to flood our senses. Even the air here is different. Go on, take a sniff.

MICHAEL: *(a small sniff)* I don't smell anything.

BUXTON: And they say you're sensitive. Come on, sniff with my nose.

They both sniff together.

There. Can't you smell it now?

Michael looks confused.

Life! Adventure! A banquet for the soul.

MICHAEL: Sometimes I don't follow you, Buxton.

BUXTON: Follow me you shall, Davies. Until you smell what I smell. Until you see what I see. Until you feel what I feel. Come on, let's not waste any more precious moments.

Michael runs after him.

MICHAEL: Wait! You've forgotten the wine.

Scene 8

Michael and Buxton on the banks of the Seine. They are sharing the bread and wine. Before each sip, Michael wipes the lip of the bottle while Buxton just quaffs it down.

MICHAEL: This is terribly decadent, Buxton.

BUXTON: Tell me, how does James Barrie come to be your uncle?

MICHAEL: He isn't really any relation at all. We just call him uncle. It's a habit we got into when I was very young. You see, my father died when I was seven and not long after my mother died.

BUXTON: How romantic.

MICHAEL: I can scarcely remember them at all any more. I have a miniature of both of them but when I look at it they're like two people I can't put a character to.

BUXTON: That way you can spin all sorts of fantasies around their memory.

MICHAEL: My older brothers often speak of them but they're not talking about two people I remember.

BUXTON: I still don't understand the connection with Uncle Jim.

MICHAEL: Kensington Gardens. Uncle Jim used to see my brothers there when our nanny took them for a walk. That's how Peter Pan came about. Based on my brothers. And with each revival a little more on me after I was born. My brother Peter remembers it didn't take Uncle Jim long to ingratiate himself with my mother.

BUXTON: Were they in love?

MICHAEL: No, I don't think so. Uncle Jim was married.

BUXTON: How delicious if they were.

MICHAEL: Peter tells me that father was jealous for a time but came to realise Uncle Jim's intentions were strictly honorable. He did get a little jealous of Uncle Jim's hold over us, though. But, in the end, when father was sick, he was glad of Uncle Jim's support. Financial as well as physical.

BUXTON: Do you miss them frightfully?

MICHAEL: Would it shock you if I said 'no'?

BUXTON: It wouldn't shock me, it would delight me. I think one's parents should be forgotten like yesterday's newspapers.

MICHAEL: Absolute twaddle, Buxton.

MICHAEL: Besides, your Uncle Jim sounds like an altogether fine substitute. I should really like to meet him.

MICHAEL: Really?

BUXTON: Of course. Who doesn't want to meet the country's most successful playwright?

MICHAEL: Don't you find his writing… quaint?

BUXTON: Who said so?

MICHAEL: Bassett finds his works too little about real life.

BUXTON: And what would Bassett know of real life?

MICHAEL: Uncle Jim has asked that you call on him whenever you like. He wants to thank you personally for standing up for his reputation though he thinks it needs little standing up for.

BUXTON: But those who earn their livelihood from public approbation must guard jealously against the tarnish of gossip. Once begun, gossip can spread like the Fire of London and leave as much destruction in its wake.

MICHAEL: I thought you didn't care about gossip or reputation.

BUXTON: Nor do I. To prove it I shall swim in the Seine in my underclothes.

MICHAEL: No, Buxton, you mustn't. You'll be arrested. There'll be an awful fuss.

BUXTON: *(stripping)* Come on, join me. It's not very deep.

MICHAEL: No, Buxton, no. I can't swim. And the current looks awfully strong.

BUXTON: Then you shall be my life saver if I get into difficulties.

MICHAEL: Please, I beg you, don't. Please. For me.

BUXTON: Didn't I say the only way to unspoil you was to refuse to do what you want?

MICHAEL: You've made your point, Buxton. So please don't.

BUXTON: Too late, Davies. I'm off.

Buxton plunges into the Seine.

MICHAEL: Don't go too far. Stay where I can see you.

BUXTON: *(voice off)* Come on, Davies. Come on in.

MICHAEL: Stay where I can see you, Buxton.

Michael watches anxiously.

Buxton? Buxton, don't play games... Where are you? Please don't play silly games... Buxton, answer me. Answer me, Buxton. My god. Buxton! Buxton! Buxton! Help somebody! Au secours! Buxton is drowning! I can't see Buxton! Anybody!

Realising there is no help about, Michael begins to remove his clothing as if he is about to plunge into the river. Buxton clambers out unseen by Michael.

BUXTON: That was refreshing.

MICHAEL: *(surprised)* Buxton! I thought you were drowned.

BUXTON: Not me. I'm a champion swimmer.

He dresses.

MICHAEL: I will never forgive you for that.

BUXTON: Were you going to jump in after me?

MICHAEL: I thought you were in difficulty.

BUXTON: If you're going to be so foolhardy then I had better teach you to swim. Why, Davies, you're trembling. Whatever is the matter?

MICHAEL: Bastard!

BUXTON: You really are upset. Look, I'm awfully sorry. I always seem to be upsetting you. Here, let me make it up to you.

MICHAEL: You can't.

BUXTON: Well, let me try at least.

MICHAEL: How?

BUXTON: Have you ever made love in Paris?

MICHAEL: Buxton!

BUXTON: I see not. There's nothing more invigorating than lovemaking as the sun comes up on a new day. And in what better city than Paris to have your first experience at dawn.

MICHAEL: I don't really...

BUXTON: Don't be shy, Davies. Come along.

MICHAEL: But, Senhouse? Bassett?

BUXTON: Let them find their own.

Searching his pockets.

I have just enough for the two of us and I know just the place.

MICHAEL: You mean a whore?

BUXTON: Of course, what did you think I meant?

MICHAEL: I don't think this is a good idea at all, Buxton.

BUXTON: It will make our friendship stronger.

Buxton puts his arm around Michael's shoulder.

Scene 9

Buxton is talking quietly to a PROSTITUTE leaning against a wall. Michael is watching, terrified. Buxton counts out his money and calls to Michael.

BUXTON: I say, Davies, this is frightfully bad form but can you spare a few francs? I don't seem to have enough money for the both of us.

MICHAEL: Don't worry about me, Buxton. You go ahead. I left all my money with Senhouse.

BUXTON: Can't do that, old chap. This is to say sorry for scaring you back there.

Digging deeper into his pockets.

Don't need it, Davies. Just found some more in the lining.

He counts the money and gives it to the Prostitute who also counts it. She motions to the two of them to follow her.

This will be such great fun, Davies. Making love is an art form to the French.

MICHAEL: What about disease, Buxton?

BUXTON: They say you're not a real man until you've had the clap at least once. And with modern medicine the way it is, why, you're cured in no time.

MICHAEL: Where are we going?

BUXTON: No idea! That's half the fun. *(pointing)* Oh, look. The sun. How grand!

MICHAEL: I'll just meet you back at the pensione.

BUXTON: Buck up, Davies. I've just paid her my last francs and she won't give them back. You'll have to make the most of it now. She asked if we wanted to do it together.

MICHAEL: What?

BUXTON: Such refreshing openness. Can you imagine our English roses even knowing what to do let alone two at time?

MICHAEL: That's disgusting!

BUXTON: Hasn't Paris taught you anything?

MICHAEL: A lot more than I care to know.

PROSTITUTE: Come, we are here.

They enter a pokey little room.

MICHAEL: My God! There's only one room.

PROSTITUTE: *(bored)* Zat is all we need in Paree. Oo is first?

Buxton pushes Michael toward her.

BUXTON: Off you go then.

MICHAEL: Here? Now? In front of you?

BUXTON: Whatever is the matter with you, Davies? I can't lounge about in the hallway.

The Prostitute strips to her corset.

PROSTITUTE: I 'aven't got all day.

She grabs Buxton.

If your friend is a little shy why not show 'im 'ow it is done.

BUXTON: Davies, it's only manners that you go first.

PROSTITUTE: You English are so polite. But also so very slow. Must I do everything for you?

She is undoing Buxton's trousers.

You are so young and 'andsome. You will almost be a plaisir.

MICHAEL: I don't feel terribly well, Buxton.

BUXTON: You're just a little lightheaded from all that red wine. Sit down a moment. I shan't be too long here.

PROSTITUTE: Your friend, 'e likes to watch, non?

MICHAEL: No! I do not!

PROSTITUTE: Je ne suis pas jolie, peut-etre?

Buxton begins to have sex with her.

BUXTON: Now you've hurt her feelings, Davies.

MICHAEL: Buxton, she's a whore.

PROSTITUTE: Per'aps I am not good enough for you, my pretty young friend. Mais personne ne s'est plaint jusqu'a present.

BUXTON: He meant no offence.

Buxton groans with pleasure. The Prostitute motions to Michael to join in. Michael is simultaneously fascinated and repelled.

I say, Davies, she's a little stunner.

PROSTITUTE: The Englishman is nervous. I will cure 'im of that. Come closer, mon petit, let me make you a man. Un homme, un vrai.

MICHAEL: This is wrong, Buxton. Terribly wrong.

BUXTON: Not now, Davies. Not now, for heaven's sake.

PROSTITUTE: *(to Michael)* Your friend is very strong, tu sais. Very ... powerful! Good husband for a woman.

MICHAEL: Stop it, Buxton. I don't want this.

PROSTITUTE: Ton copain, c'est un puceau, ou quoi?

BUXTON: Are you, Davies? Are you a virgin?

PROSTITUTE: 'E is watching us like a virgin. Non, 'e is watching us like a jealous lover. *(addressing Michael)* Sais pas si presse, l'ami. It will soon be your turn.

MICHAEL: I don't want a turn. Come on, Buxton, let's leave now!

Michael tugs at Buxton who is groaning and who is certainly not about to stop. Michael is begging while Buxton merely continues his action groaning contentedly and the Prostitute begins to laugh at the farcical situation. It continues as lights fade.

Scene 10

Barrie addresses the audience.

BARRIE: So, now he is sated with Paris, indeed, seems to actively dislike the city, and to make amends and give him the benefit of clear-minded Scottish air we are soon to journey north for a holiday with Nico and some of Michael's friends. We are headed for Eilean Shona, an idyllic little island at the entrance to Loch Moidart on the coast of Argyll. There will be no one on the island but us in one rambling house, miles from civilisation. It will be nice to have the boys around me, they keep me young. It will not be quite so nice, however, to have as an uninvited guest, my former wife, Mary Ansell, come, no doubt, to beg charity from her cuckolded husband.

Scene 11

Michael, Senhouse, Bassett, and Nico, en route to Eilean Shona.

BASSETT: Don't you get tired of this annual trek to Scotland to be at Uncle Jim's beck and call?

MICHAEL: It's a small price to pay for what he's done for us. Right, Nico?

NICO: Anyway, we like the fishing.

SENHOUSE: Ugh!

BASSETT: Why is it, Senhouse, that you have such an aversion to anything which requires any sort of physical exertion?

SENHOUSE: Precisely because it is physical. And not of the mind.

MICHAEL: Come on, Senhouse. Not everything can be intellectual.

SENHOUSE: Name something!

MICHAEL: Love!

SENHOUSE: Ah, yes, but it begins as an intellectual exercise.

MICHAEL: Not always.

SENHOUSE: Anyway, I consider you to be biased, Davies major, and therefore take no notice of your arguments.

MICHAEL: What bias?

SENHOUSE: Your proficiency at cricket makes your arguments ineligible. Bassett, here, at least has the decency to play all games very badly.

NICO: Uncle Jim will expect you to join in the cricket, Senhouse.

MICHAEL: And you will unless you want to be on the receiving end of one of his moods.

SENHOUSE: All that incessant talk of Test matches with the Australians. We could have gone back to Paris and stayed at a proper hotel this time.

MICHAEL: I never want to see Paris again as long as I live. It's a wretched city.

BASSETT: I wish you'd tell us what happened to turn you against Paris so suddenly. But, at least, we won't have to put up with that pompous Buxton character.

NICO: Does this mean you'll be going to Oxford after all, Michael?

MICHAEL: I haven't made up my mind yet.

NICO: Please say you will. Then I shall have a friend when I finish Eton and go to Oxford myself.

SENHOUSE: I thought you'd have a lot of friends, Nico.

NICO: Few to speak of. I shall miss not having Michael around.

MICHAEL: You'll get to like it, Nico. I did. Almost.

SENHOUSE: We had some good times at Eton.

MICHAEL: Sorry, Senhouse. You were one of the bright spots of my years there. And you too, Bassett.

NICO: Michael, do you tell Uncle Jim everything?

MICHAEL: No, not everything. He doesn't expect that.

NICO: Anyway I shall be in big trouble with Uncle Jim.

MICHAEL: Oh?

NICO: The master of my college is writing to him. I'm afraid of what he will say.

MICHAEL: There can never be anything so terrible you can't tell Uncle Jim.

NICO: *(plucking up the courage to talk about it)* It's about me going about with a smaller boy named Wright. He's under two years younger than me and a good bit lower in the school. My tutor says it does both him and me harm, but I'll never believe that.

Michael and Senhouse exchange knowing glances.

MICHAEL: Unless you are leading each other into bad language or bad ways I can't see that Uncle Jim will see any mischief.

NICO: The chief reason I go about with Wright so often, and it's the only reason, is that I like him better than anyone in my tutor's. He's good looking and because of that my tutor says I am, so to speak, in love with him.

SENHOUSE: And are you, Nico?

NICO: Of course not, it's just perfectly natural friendship.

Bassett attempts desperately to change the subject.

BASSETT: Where is this ruddy place we're supposed to bury ourselves in for weeks?

NICO: *(pointing)* There it is. Over there.

SENHOUSE: That? That is where we are meant to spend a glorious few weeks of what is supposed to be the years in which we mis-spend our youth?

MICHAEL: It's not very prepossessing, is it?

BASSETT: This does not auger well, Davies. All we need now is a thunderstorm to make the atmosphere complete.

MICHAEL: It's like something out of a Bram Stoker novel.

NICO: I think it looks spiffing.

Barrie enters.

Uncle Jim! Uncle Jim!

BARRIE: Nico. And gentlemen, welcome to Eilean Shona. *(almost shyly)* Hello, Michael. *(shaking hands)* Mr Senhouse, as I remember. And Mr Bassett. No Mr Buxton?

MICHAEL: He'd already made other arrangements, Uncle Jim.

BARRIE: No doubt he will be missed. But we shall still have a wonderful time. Plenty of cricket *(Senhouse winces)* and wonderful trout fishing. And no one to disturb the tranquillity of the place.

NICO: How do we get to the island, Uncle Jim? Do we all have to swim?

BARRIE: Of course not.

Picking up a handful of earth.

I merely sprinkle a little fairy dust on us and we fly over like Peter Pan and Wendy.

He sprinkles a little on Nico and goes to do the same to the others but they move away almost imperceptibly. Barrie drops the soil and brushes his hands clean.

Well, perhaps not.

(to Michael) You would have believed once.

MICHAEL: A long time ago, Uncle Jim.

BARRIE: A pity you should ever grow to disbelieve. But you young gentlemen must be tired and hungry, so let's away. There's a launch waiting to take us all across. It's our only contact with the outside world and we must use it for the mail and to gather our provisions. As you see, we are almost totally cut off up here.

BASSETT: It seems barely civilised.

NICO: Oh, Michael, come and see. It looks rather like Captain Hook's pirate ship.

BARRIE: A little small for pirates, Nico. But if your imagination can transform a simple launch into a pirate ship who am I to argue?

MICHAEL: Are we to travel to the island on that?

BARRIE: How else? You rejected my alternative method.

MICHAEL: Is it safe?

SENHOUSE: Do pull yourself together, Davies.

BARRIE: I'm afraid you must carry your own bags. Michael, I will take yours.

He picks up Michael's bag and exits while Michael stands staring at the water. Senhouse comes to him.

SENHOUSE: Bassett, give me a hand will you?

BASSETT: What is it?

SENHOUSE: Davies major is in a bit of a funk. *(to Michael)* Come on, old chap.

Barrie returns.

BARRIE: Is anything the matter?

SENHOUSE: Just over tired. It's been a long journey.

Senhouse and Bassett manoeuvre Michael toward the boat as we hear the sound of lapping water.

Scene 12

Barrie addresses the audience as MARY ANSELL has breakfast in the background.

BARRIE: We have been on the island for a few days, and a wild romantic isle it is, too. It almost takes the breath away to find so perfectly appointed a retreat on these untamed shores. This is a very lovely spot, almost painfully so, and for a work room I have chosen one where I can hide from the scenery but, alas, not from the noises of youth.

Buxton struggles on with his suitcase looking a trifle lost.

BUXTON: I say, I am in the right place?

MARY: It's hard to say. Where had you intended being at this precise moment?

BUXTON: Some godforsaken island called Eilean Shona.

MARY: Then, indeed, you are in the right place.

BUXTON: I didn't know there were going to be other guests here.

MARY: I'm what's known as a last minute cast change.

BUXTON: You're in the theatre!

MARY: I was.

BUXTON: Was?

MARY: I gave it up when I married James.

BUXTON: Aha! You're Mary Ansell. Uncle Jim's former wife.

MARY: *(amused)* Uncle Jim? You call him Uncle Jim?

BUXTON: I'm embarrassed to say I have never met Mr Barrie.

MARY: *(deliberately repeating his exclamation)* Aha! Then you must be the presumptuous Mr Buxton.

BUXTON: Forgive me. My natural inquisitiveness is sometimes mistaken for presumption.

MARY: *(nods her forgiveness)* You are not expected.

BUXTON: I hope I am not unwelcome though?

MARY: Your absence has hung over this holiday like a ghost. That, of course, makes you immeasurably more interesting. You have a lot to live up to.

BUXTON: *(pleased)* I have been missed then?

MARY: Would you like some coffee, Mr Buxton?

BUXTON: That would be grand. I haven't eaten all night. The train and then having to find a fisherman who would bring me over. But what extraordinary scenery.

MARY: Your coffee, Mr Buxton. Please feel free to help yourself to breakfast. The others have not come down yet so there is plenty.

BUXTON: *(sipping his coffee)* Ah, magnificent.

MARY: You are extravagant with your praise, Mr Buxton. I never used to drink coffee but I now live in Paris...

BUXTON: Ah, Paris.

MARY: Their tea is undrinkable. So one is reduced to drinking coffee. Now I have become so used to it I find tea tastes like washing up water. Not that I have ever tasted washing up water. But it tastes like I imagine washing up water would taste should you ever be silly enough to drink it.

BUXTON: Are you here on holidays, too?

MARY: I have come to throw myself on James's generosity. Since I divorced my second husband, Mr Cannan...

BUXTON: Divorce is ever so modern.

MARY: But, alas, still frowned upon. That is why my dogs are my greatest companions.

BUXTON: How sad.

MARY: Not at all, Mr Buxton. I'm perfectly happy. They make admirable companions. And I have my decorative enamel work.

BUXTON: You are still an artist then?

MARY: Of sorts. With a little of the money James settled on me...

BUXTON: If this is too personal...

MARY: By no means, Mr Buxton. It was in all the newspapers at the time. James can't do anything without it being reported. So, I managed to turn what is essentially a hobby into a thriving cottage industry. Enough to live comfortably but frugally. Then the war came...

BUXTON: You lost everything?

MARY: There's not a great demand for decorative enamel work in times of war. Beauty is one of the first casualties of conflict. But that's the way things are sometimes.

Michael enters with Senhouse and Bassett.

BUXTON: So, when do you want your first swimming lesson, Davies?

MICHAEL: *(flustered)* Buxton! How? When?

BUXTON: Where and why, anything is done and how much? And have you been practising your arithmetical tables as well, Davies?

MICHAEL: *(whispers to Buxton)* I don't know that I should be speaking to you.

Michael kisses Mary on the cheek.

Good morning, Mary.

MARY: Michael. Mr Senhouse, Mr Bassett. Please, join us for breakfast.

BASSETT: Staying long, Buxton?

BUXTON: As long as I'm welcome.

BASSETT: In that case, a very short stay indeed.

SENHOUSE: I warn you, you'll be dreadfully bored.

MARY: How can you say that, Mr Senhouse? There's so much to do here.

SENHOUSE: And so much physical energy required in the doing of it.

BASSETT: And you have Mr Barrie's cricket match to look forward to today.

SENHOUSE: I have a headache. Tell him I'm too ill.

BUXTON: The exercise will do you good, Senhouse.

SENHOUSE: Don't you start, Buxton.

MARY: Coffee, anyone?

She pours for them.

BUXTON: So, what have you been doing since you arrived?

SENHOUSE: Picnics.

MICHAEL: Hiking.

BASSETT: Fishing.

SENHOUSE: In between all this excitement, Michael has been doing some sketching.

BUXTON: Sketching? How marvellous. I'd very much like to see your work.

MICHAEL: It's only scribble.

MARY: Don't be so modest, Michael. Your work is very good.

Senhouse nods agreement.

We're not the only ones to think so.

MICHAEL: Uncle Jim thinks it's scribble.

BASSETT: What would he know?

BUXTON: Perhaps you'll sketch me some time. I'll gladly pay you for it.

MICHAEL: No. I do it for the experience, not for the money.

MARY/BUXTON: As the actress said to the bishop.

General laughter. Barrie enters.

BARRIE: Ah, there you all are! I thought I heard laughter.

MARY: Your young men have been entertaining me.

BARRIE: And very successfully by the sounds of it. Ah, I see Mr Buxton has finally arrived. Welcome.

They shake hands.

BUXTON: It's a pleasure to meet you, Mr Barrie.

MICHAEL: You knew he was coming?

BARRIE: Of course. I do keep some secrets from you, Michael. Mr Buxton wrote me a most charming letter apologising for his tardiness and asking if he might still visit. Naturally, I said he could. In fact, I insisted he visit.

BUXTON: None of you looks pleased to see me.

SENHOUSE: Of course we are, Buxton. It's just such a surprise it's taken the wind out of our sails. Right, Bassett?

BASSETT: *(not pleased at all)* Mm.

BARRIE: Michael, perhaps you would like to show Mr Buxton to his room. That way you can chat before the cricket match.

BUXTON: There's to be a game? I hope there's a spot for me?

BARRIE: I assumed you would want to rest after your long journey.

BUXTON: Who can rest when there's the sound of red ball against willow?

BARRIE: Splendidly put, Mr Buxton. Simply splendid. Shall we say in an hour then?

Buxton nods gracefully.

Well, off you go, Michael.

MICHAEL: If it's all the same, I'd rather get in a few practise shots. I'm a little rusty.

MARY: I'll show Mr Buxton to his room, James. I'm to be umpire so there's no need for me on the pitch just yet.

BARRIE: As you wish.

MARY: This way, Mr Buxton.

BARRIE: We'll get a chance to speak later, Mr Buxton.

BUXTON: I look forward to it. Au revoir.

Michael flinches at the reminder of Paris. Mary and Buxton exit.

BARRIE: A charming man, Michael. Your descriptions don't do him the justice he deserves.

MICHAEL: Mm. Come on Senhouse, Bassett. Let's pitch a few for practise.

Scene 13

Barrie addresses the audience.

BARRIE: Man's most pleasant invention is the lawnmower. All the birds know this, and that is why, when it is at rest, there is at least one of them sitting on the handle with its head cocked, wondering how the delicious whirring sound is made. When they find out, they will change their note to imitate it. As it is, you must sometimes have thought that you heard the mower very early in the morning, and perhaps you peeped from your lattice window to see who was up so early. It was really the birds trying to get the note. On this overcast morning, however, it is almost noon, and the whirring is being done by Mr Buxton. He is making the lawn ready for our game of cricket. He has all the energy of a young man possessed by his own youth. And that's as it should be. He tells me that as well as adventure he is looking for love. Ah, I tell him, I once went looking for love which, perhaps because of nearsightedness, I did not see, or at least, I did not recognise.

Scene 14

Preparing for the cricket match.

SENHOUSE: I really don't know how I let you talk me into this.

NICO: It's just to make up the numbers, Senhouse.

SENHOUSE: No one will want me on their team. It's always the way.

MICHAEL: You can play for our side, Senhouse.

SENHOUSE: That's awfully decent of you, Davies. I know you'd much rather have Buxton.

MICHAEL: For heaven's sake, it's only a game.

NICO: Not to Uncle Jim. For him cricket is a way of life.

SENHOUSE: *(frustrated)* Cream has never been my color.

BASSETT: Don't play the silly ass, Senhouse.

Barrie enters.

BARRIE: Righto, are we all ready? This is going to be a Test match in the true spirit of cricket. My team, of course, shall be the English, and Michael's team shall be the Australians.

NICO: Oh! Can I be on your side, Michael, can I? The Australians are so jolly good.

MICHAEL: That's Senhouse and Nico on my team. That leaves you with Buxton and Bassett, Uncle Jim.

BARRIE: And delighted to have you we are too, Mr Bassett.

SENHOUSE: Where's Buxton?

BARRIE: Out checking the pitch. A most conscientious young man.

Lights dim to signal the cricket match. When lights come up, Buxton is batting and Barrie is running from the opposite end. Nico is bowling and Michael is wicket keeper. Senhouse is the forlorn fielder. Mary is umpire. She gives the signal for Nico to bowl and Buxton hits it solidly. There is a groan from Senhouse.

MICHAEL: Come on, Senhouse, put your back into it!

SENHOUSE: *(barely audible)* Balls.

BUXTON: What was that, Senhouse?

SENHOUSE: I said I hate to go running after balls.

BUXTON: Your reputation says otherwise.

Senhouse glares at Buxton but the others have not heard the exchange.

MICHAEL: Well, go after it, man.

Senhouse goes after the ball.

BUXTON: Senhouse. Bit of a sissy.

MICHAEL: He just doesn't like cricket. It's not everyone's cup of tea, after all.

BUXTON: What sort of man is it doesn't like the world's most civilised game?

MICHAEL: Senhouse, for one.

BUXTON: Exactly my point.

MICHAEL: Be careful. Senhouse is my friend.

BUXTON: Yes, I heard talk.

Senhouse comes back on with the ball. He throws it to Nico and then lies down puffing.

MARY: That was four. Well done, Mr Buxton.

SENHOUSE: You can run after your own ruddy ball in future. I really can't see any point to it.

BARRIE: The point, my dear Mr Senhouse, is to route your opposition.

SENHOUSE: I thought this was a sporting competition for gentlemen.

BUXTON: Cricket prepares you for life. It trains the eye to concentrate on the minutia while simultaneously taking in the grand view. Right, Mr Barrie?

BARRIE: Excellently put, Mr Buxton. You have the soul of a true cricketer.

SENHOUSE: What do you think, Davies?

MICHAEL: It's only a game. One I just happen to be good at.

SENHOUSE: Well, all I see when I watch a game of cricket is a lot of silly men tossing...

NICO: Bowling, Senhouse.

SENHOUSE: A lot of silly men bowling…

Nico nods his approval.

…a red ball at another lot of silly men at the other end of the...

NICO: Pitch!

SENHOUSE: Pitch who try to whack it into eternity. Hardly the stuff of great philosophical moment.

BUXTON: That's it, Senhouse. The Philosophy of Cricket.

SENHOUSE: I hadn't realised Socrates played cricket.

BARRIE: Are we going to get on with the game? The English are winning for a change and I'd hate to see the game called a draw because of lack of light.

MARY: Change of bowlers, please. Nico has had his turn.

NICO: Oh, Mary. And I gave you a shilling to let me stay on.

MARY: The umpire's behaviour must be seen to be above reproach.

NICO: Then can I have my shilling back please?

MARY: Of course not. That will teach you never to attempt to bribe an umpire.

BARRIE: You young scoundrel.

MICHAEL: Would you like to take a turn at bowling, Senhouse?

BUXTON: Not again, Davies. The chap's a chucker.

SENHOUSE: No thanks, you do it. I'll just lie here and watch the balls fly by.

MICHAEL: Come on, Nico. You be wicket keeper.

Michael and Nico change ends and Michael bowls to Buxton who easily plays it. The game continues with Michael bowling to Barrie who hits the ball equally as skillfully. Buxton waits for Michael to retrieve the ball.

BUXTON: So, how do you get on with your brother, Nico? I can call you Nico?

NICO: Of course, Buxton. Please. I think you're super. The nicest friend Michael's ever brought home.

BUXTON: Has he brought home many friends?

NICO: Mainly Senhouse and Bassett. And sometimes, Marjoribanks.

BUXTON: Oh?

Michael returns with the ball.

MICHAEL: Well fielded, Senhouse.

MARY: See how he stands with the bat at the ready. His gaze never deviates from the ball. He's like an ancient Celtic warrior.

SENHOUSE: Arrogant! Self-satisfied! Anyway, I doubt the ancient Celts wore cricket pads.

MARY: They would have if they'd had them.

BASSETT: Come on, Buxton, whack the ruddy thing like you're famous for.

Michael bowls and Buxton is almost out.

MARY: Oh, well played, Mr Buxton.

BARRIE: The umpire is supposed to remain strictly impartial, Mary.

SENHOUSE: Don't encourage him, his arrogance is already monumental.

MICHAEL: I'll get you next time, Buxton.

BUXTON: Not a chance, Davies.

Michael runs up to bowl just as Buxton begins humming 'La Marseillaise'. It throws Michael off and he bowls badly.

MARY: It's a wide.

BASSETT: You are out of form, Davies. We shall walk all over you and your team.

SENHOUSE: No fair humming, Buxton.

BUXTON: Show me in the rules where it says a fellow can't hum. Aren't I right, umpire?

MARY: Correct, Mr Buxton.

BARRIE: You're making up these rules as you go along, Mary.

MARY: Makes the game more interesting, don't you think?

BASSETT: You can't make up your own rules. You have to play the game.

Mary signals Michael to bowl and Buxton hits it for two.

BUXTON: Come on, Davies, where's this great skill I heard you possess? Lose it in Paris?

Michael fumbles again and is getting angry at being ragged by Buxton. Senhouse begins to take more interest in the game now that Paris has been mentioned.

NICO: You can do better than that, Michael. Bowl the blighter out.

BUXTON: Yes, Davies, bowl me out. Show me what you're made of.

Hums 'La Marseillaise' again as Michael bowls. Michael deliberately aims the ball at Buxton's groin which it hits with a resounding thump.

MARY: Are you badly hurt?

SENHOUSE: Good shot, Davies. I think I could get to like cricket after all.

The sound of thunder.

BARRIE: *(looking up)* Hmph. Not very convincing. You can do a lot better than that.

MICHAEL: I think play might be over for the day. Because of bad light.

MARY: Back to the house everyone. It's become very overcast.

NICO: Come on, I'll race you all back.

Only Bassett takes him on.

BARRIE: Are you all right, Mr Buxton?

BUXTON: Just a little bump. Nothing to worry over really.

BARRIE: We'll have a proper look at it when we get back. Pity it had to end like this. Michael is usually such a reliable bowler.

BUXTON: He still is.

Rain begins to fall and everyone runs for shelter. Buxton, though, is obviously in more pain than he is letting on. Michael is gathering up the last of the cricket gear.

SENHOUSE: That was the best shot of the day, Davies. Well done!

Runs for the house.

BUXTON: A few inches to the right and I would have been neutered.

MICHAEL: It was an option I considered.

Buxton limps in great pain.

BUXTON: Ah!

MICHAEL: If you expect me to make a fuss over a little bump then you're sadly mistaken.

BUXTON: Then you don't believe I'm injured?

MICHAEL: Of course not. Your whole life is a pretence.

BUXTON: Then you don't realise your own strength. Why do you think I came all the way to this godforsaken place?

MICHAEL: To continue a very poor joke at my expense.

BUXTON: You are thick sometimes, Davies.

MICHAEL: Senhouse and Bassett were right about you.

BUXTON: Now you have offended me.

MICHAEL: I liked you, Buxton. But you let me down.

Michael runs off, leaving Buxton to hobble after him.

BUXTON: Wait up, Davies. That's why I'm here. I like you, too. *(shouting)* Dammit! I really like you!

END OF ACT ONE

Act Two

Scene 1

James Barrie addresses the audience.

BARRIE: I suppose I always knew I created Peter Pan by rubbing the five Llewelyn Davies boys violently together, as savages with two sticks produce a flame. That was all he was - the spark I got from them. And after I had conjured him from the flames I found myself the subject of my own early fairy stories waiting for the boys to set me free. But now, instead, I find myself trapped more and more than ever in my own Never Land by my affection for Michael. Never Land is that place everyone seeks in childhood but finds only in dreams and imagination. I fancy I tried to create an imaginary world for myself because the one I really inhabit, and the only one I can do any good in, is too sombre. I have been having a bout of this depressing kind since we landed on Eilean Shona and I have little to show for it but a severe philosophic countenance.

Scene 2

A few days later. Bassett is fishing for trout while Michael is sketching Senhouse.

MICHAEL: If you don't stand still, Senhouse, I can't possibly capture you in pencil or charcoal.

SENHOUSE: I'm so terribly bored, Davies. Even the cricket match had more excitement than this. We daren't go near the house for fear of stumbling on another financial discussion between Mary and Uncle Jim or else we get shooed away because Buxton is monopolising the old man.

BASSETT: We didn't come here to spend all our time in the house.

MICHAEL: Besides, it's their affair, not ours.

SENHOUSE: I'd be more than happy if there were any affairs for us on this island. But it's so bleak and devoid of affection the goats are beginning to look attractive.

MICHAEL: For god's sake, Senhouse, be still!

SENHOUSE: What about you? You've been so snappy and irritable since Uncle Jim monopolised Buxton. Hasn't he, Bassett?

BASSETT: I thought he was supposed to be your friend, Davies.

SENHOUSE: You've been provoking arguments over every petty little thing and keep them going long after you should have given it away and made amends. The atmosphere around here is like porridge.

MICHAEL: I'm sorry Senhouse, Bassett. It hasn't been much fun.

SENHOUSE: The one saving grace has been Mary.

BASSETT: When she can tear herself away from her fiscal finagling.

MICHAEL: I say, why don't we invite her for a picnic?

SENHOUSE: Where?

MICHAEL: There's a lovely little spot not far from here. And she hasn't seen much of the island yet.

SENHOUSE: That sounds splendid. What do you say, Bassett?

BASSETT: Sounds a good deal better than standing here trying to convince the trout I'm any sort of a fisherman.

MICHAEL: Why don't you two go and make the arrangements and bring Mary and Nico back here.

SENHOUSE: We'll do our best.

BASSETT: Aren't you coming?

MICHAEL: I want to stay as far away from the house as possible for the time being.

SENHOUSE: Oh, all right.

MICHAEL: Don't forget to bring some chocolate cake with you.

SENHOUSE: What picnic would be complete without chocolate cake? Coming, Bassett?

BASSETT: Coming. See you soon, Davies.

Michael calls after them as they leave.

MICHAEL: **S**hould you pass any attractive goats on your journey, then invite them along.

Sounds of laughter. Buxton enters behind Michael and ensures the others have left. He throws a stone at Michael who does not turn around.

MICHAEL: Cut it out!

Buxton throws another stone and bleats like a goat. Michael turns. He is not pleased to see Buxton.

Oh, it's you.

BUXTON: What about that swimming lesson, Davies?

MICHAEL: I didn't bring a bathing costume.

BUXTON: No matter. There's no one to see you.

MICHAEL: Why are you doing this, Buxton?

Buxton ignores the question and goes to remove his bathing costume.

BUXTON: You can borrow mine if you like.

Michael is horrified.

MICHAEL: What would you wear?

BUXTON: It's perfectly natural. We were born that way.

MICHAEL: You wouldn't.

Buxton prepares to leave.

BUXTON: I can see I'm wasting my time here.

MICHAEL: I know. Let me sketch you.

BUXTON: So the day's not wasted after all.

Buxton strikes a silly pose.

How do you want me?

MICHAEL: No, not like that. Something noble. Warrior like.

Buxton poses again.

No, that's not quite it.

Posing perfectly.

BUXTON: Like this then?

MICHAEL: Perfect! Can you hold that pose for a while?

BUXTON: Of course. I can do anything I set my mind to.

MICHAEL: Let me know when you want a rest.

BUXTON: Will this take terribly long?

MICHAEL: It might. If I do it properly.

BUXTON: Well, we have all afternoon.

MICHAEL: Try to keep still if you can. Perfectly still.

BUXTON: Am I allowed to speak, Davies?

MICHAEL: As long as you don't move your mouth.

Michael becomes absorbed in sketching.

BUXTON: How's it going?

MICHAEL: I've scarcely begun, Buxton. Have a little patience. You've the most exquisite profile I've ever sketched.

BUXTON: Then don't talk about it. Get it down on paper.

Michael sketches a while longer and then in a fit of frustration scrawls across what his efforts.

BUXTON: I sense all is not well in the world of fine art.

MICHAEL: There's something dreadfully wrong. I don't know...

BUXTON: Give me a look.

Buxton goes over to Michael to examine the sketch but Michael attempts to hide it.

What am I supposed to be?

MICHAEL: *(mumbling)* An heroic Celtic warrior.

BUXTON: A what?

MICHAEL: An heroic Celtic warrior.

BUXTON: Is that how you see me?

MICHAEL: *(reluctantly)* Yes.

BUXTON: Why didn't you say so? I know what the problem is.

Removing his bathers and standing naked.

Celtic warriors never wore bathers.

He strikes his pose again.

68

There, that should be a great deal better.

MICHAEL: Buxton, you can't just...what if someone… Put your clothes on! Buxton, I've never been so shocked.

BUXTON: Davies, if you don't pick up that pencil of yours and start drawing within ten seconds I'm going to put my clothes on and go home. I'm freezing my balls off standing like this.

Michael hurriedly takes up his pencil and begins to sketch nervously.

MICHAEL: You're quite right, it is better like this.

BUXTON: Quite. I may know nothing about art but I do know how to pose.

Sounds of people approaching.

MICHAEL: There's someone coming. Quick! Hide! Put your clothes on!

Buxton doesn't move.

BUXTON: Have you finished the sketch?

MICHAEL: No, but...

BUXTON: Then finish it.

Barrie, Nico, Mary, Senhouse, and Bassett enter.

SENHOUSE: My god! Buxton!

MARY: Mon dieu. There's a sight you don't often see while walking the Scottish Highlands.

BASSETT: Put your clothes on, Buxton. There's a lady present. Have you no shame?

BUXTON: As a matter of fact, none. What do you say, Mr Barrie?

BARRIE: *(amused)* I think you must be very cold.

MICHAEL: Put your clothes on, Buxton!

BARRIE: Perhaps if we adjourn to that idyllic little spot just downstream we can set up and wait for the great artist to finish. Then he and Mr Buxton can join us. This way everyone.

Nico is staring.

Come on, Nico.

They exit.

MICHAEL: All you ever seem to do is embarrass me, Buxton.

BUXTON: What do you mean?

MICHAEL: You didn't even cover yourself.

BUXTON: Was I meant to?

MICHAEL: Don't you ever do anything that's expected of you?

BUXTON: Never! When I die I shan't be remembered as ordinary.

MICHAEL: You think that's an admirable goal to have in life?

BUXTON: Don't you have a goal?

MICHAEL: To be happy, I suppose.

BUXTON: Everyone has that as a goal. Come on, something different.

MICHAEL: I should like to fall terribly in love.

BUXTON: Damn it, Davies, can't you think of anything more adventurous than that? Don't be so wet.

MICHAEL: I can't help it, it's the way I was brought up.

BUXTON: With James Barrie as your guardian I'd have thought that would be enough to set you furiously to think.

MICHAEL: And so I do. Sometimes. Most of the time.

BUXTON: Well, what are you thinking right this very minute. Come on. Own up.

MICHAEL: I was merely thinking how much I would like it if you'd teach me to... swim.

BUXTON: By the time I've finished with you you'll be swimming like one of the trout in this stream.

MICHAEL: Please be careful, Buxton, I'm frightened to get in over my head.

BUXTON: Then we shall start out easy. In fact, we shan't even go in the water at first. Not until you gain confidence.

MICHAEL: How then can I learn?

BUXTON: I'll teach you the arm movements first. Then how to kick your legs.

Buxton demonstrates arm movements. Michael imitates.

MICHAEL: I feel such an idiot not being able to swim. All the other chaps at Eton could.

BUXTON: Soon you'll swim as well as you play cricket. Just follow my example.

MICHAEL: I am awfully glad you came, Buxton.

BUXTON: I'm awfully glad I came, too, Davies. Paris was so dull after you left. And all the other chaps at school seemed so tiresome in comparison.

MICHAEL: Though I shall never forgive you.

BUXTON: You said that once before.

MICHAEL: Then don't remind me of that city. Or my behaviour there.

BUXTON: Not even to make you angry?

MICHAEL: Not even that.

BUXTON: And, of course, you must kick your feet at the same time.

MICHAEL: Am I doing this right? Surely there's more to it than that?

BUXTON: Almost. Here, let me show you.

Buxton stands behind Michael and guides his arms as if they are participants in synchronised swimming.

MICHAEL: Is that better?

BUXTON: Notice how comfortably we fit together? I noticed it in Paris.

MICHAEL: Buxton! You promised!

BUXTON: When you waited up with that red wine and the bread. I thought, there's a chap I wouldn't mind...

MICHAEL: Go on, Buxton. Wouldn't mind what?

BUXTON: Wouldn't mind as a...special friend.

Michael stops his swimming motions and turns which means he is in Buxton's arms. Buxton continues his arm motions for a while longer and then places his hands on Michael's shoulders. Michael stands perfectly still. Buxton puts his arms around Michael. Michael allows it for a moment and then pulls away.

MICHAEL: At least life would never be ordinary or conventional.

BUXTON: In order to learn how to swim you first have to get your feet wet.

Scene 3

The picnic. Mary, Nico, Senhouse and Bassett prepare the repast. Barrie looks in the direction in which they left Michael and Buxton.

BARRIE: The modern child finds Captain Hook a grotesque figure, albeit a little comic. But, in reality, he is a tragic and rather ghastly creation who knows no peace, and whose soul is in torment. A dark shadow, a sinister dream, a bogey of fear who lives perpetually in the grey recesses of every child's mind. I am reminded of this constantly by the manner in which I am treated by Michael's young men. *(sighing)* And I feel as lonely as God.

NICO: What are you looking at, Uncle Jim?

BARRIE: I was admiring the scenery. It's so beautiful I half expected to see a postage stamp in one corner signifying it was nought but a fantastical picture postcard.

SENHOUSE: Whatever else one may say about this island the scenery is breathtaking.

BASSETT: If rivers and mountains and goats are to your liking.

NICO: Oh, do buck up, Bassett.

BASSETT: It's the damnable weather. Sunny one minute and the next the heavens open unexpectedly and quite drench us.

BARRIE: Not quite so unexpectedly, Mr Bassett. There is usually a growl of disapproval from the thunder that anyone should like sunny weather.

BASSETT: This is a foul outcrop.

BARRIE: At least when it rains I get my work done. When it's sunny it quite tempts me out of doors to exertions I should not have contemplated otherwise.

MARY: You're still a very active man, James.

BARRIE: But I am constantly reminded of my frailty on this island. Why, when I come in from a prodigious walk over mountains whose very names call for stout climbers, cheered by thoughts of modest boasting at afternoon tea, I am told by Michael or Mr Buxton that the achievement is nothing and merely the warm-up for their daily excursions when it is not raining.

NICO: Where are they? They'll miss the picnic.

BASSETT: One would hope Buxton is making himself decent. I think he owes all of us an apology. Especially Miss Ansell.

MARY: I require no apology, Mr Bassett.

SENHOUSE: Nor I.

BASSETT: He made a disgraceful exhibition of himself.

MARY: He is a very...er...virile young man.

BARRIE: I should have thought a modern young man such as yourself would have found such behaviour a lark rather than a cause for condemnation, Mr Bassett.

BASSETT: I have an impeccable sense of good and ill behaviour, Mr Barrie. It has been instilled in me from birth. I expected you would share such opinions.

BARRIE: Ah, I do so hate expectations. One can never live up to them, so I never try. And as for set opinions, Mr

Bassett, every morning, with a medium-soft brush, I clean my brain of all it has eaten the previous day.

MARY: At any rate, Mr Bassett, we are among friends. That excuses almost anything.

NICO: Does it really, Uncle Jim?

BARRIE: Of course, Nico. Friendship forgives almost anything and almost everything is forgiven in the name of friendship.

BASSETT: Except betrayal.

Mary covers her embarrassment by taking out her knitting. Barrie looks at her as he delivers the next line.

BARRIE: Even that can be forgiven with time.

Mary gives a slight nod of thanks.

BASSETT: Have you ever been betrayed by anyone close to you, Mr Barrie?

MARY: *(counting stitches)* 18. 19. 20. 21.

BARRIE: If my recollection serves me correctly...only by Michael.

NICO: Here they come. *(calling)* Hurry up you two or all the chocolate cake will be gone.

BASSETT: What kept you?

BUXTON: You have the soul of a philistine, Bassett. You can't hurry great art. It is only the best of an artist that goes into his pictures.

MARY: A man may rise above himself for an hour while under the influence of art and yet be a poor enough thing for the rest of the day.

BASSETT: *(nasty)* What devastating perception, Miss Ansell.

MICHAEL: Bassett! I apologise for Bassett's behaviour, Mary.

MARY: Why does everyone feel the need to continually apologise to me?

BASSETT: *(sarcastically)* After all, we are among friends. Anyway, it's a well known fact that women's brains weigh less than men's.

MARY: Just as sixpences weigh less than pennies, Mr Bassett.

Much mirth at Bassett's expense.

BARRIE: We have much more serious matters to which to turn our minds. *(producing a letter)* It seems young Nico here has a scandal attached to his name.

NICO: *(childishly excited)* Do I really, Uncle Jim? *(realising what he means)* Oh, you mean my friendship with Wright?

BARRIE: It seems your tutor cannot distinguish the joys of boyhood friendships from the squalor of his imagination. Do you like this Wright boy?

NICO: Very much, Uncle Jim.

BARRIE: Then friends you shall remain. You'll grow up all too soon and lose that ability to have close male contact.

BASSETT: You'd damn the tutor's well-meaning concern? You care nothing for the reputation of the boys in your care, I find that a gross dereliction of parenthood.

BARRIE: I cannot be held responsible for other people's imaginations, Mr Bassett, no matter how well intentioned. Besides, I have enough trust that they would never indulge in behaviour that would bring dishonour on themselves or those they loved.

Michael attempts to change the subject which is making him uncomfortable.

MICHAEL: Well, I'm going to have another slice of this delicious chocolate cake.

BARRIE: You will be sick tomorrow, Michael.

MICHAEL: No, Uncle Jim, I shall be sick tonight.

BUXTON: Listen, everyone. Michael has a surprise.

Buxton has used Michael's given name. Senhouse realises the import and is pleased if somewhat jealous. Bassett is shocked at Buxton's increasing influence over Michael. Mary is aware of the implications, while Barrie is peeved at the familiarity. Nico is oblivious.

NICO: How exciting. I hope it's good.

BUXTON: It's great news.

NICO: What is it, Michael. Come on, tell us.

MICHAEL: I have decided to go to Oxford after all.

SENHOUSE: That is tremendous news.

MARY: A very wise decision, Michael.

NICO: Super! Now I shall have an older brother at Oxford when I enrol there.

BASSETT: I don't know why it took you so long to make up your mind, Davies.

Barrie looks annoyed.

MICHAEL: Aren't you pleased, Uncle Jim?

BARRIE: What brought about this sudden change of heart, Michael?

MICHAEL: I thought you'd be pleased, Uncle Jim.

BARRIE: Just tell me what decided you upon this course of action.

BUXTON: I think I may have helped talk him into it, Mr Barrie.

BARRIE: Yes? Now I understand why they call you the remarkable Mr Buxton, the extraordinary Mr Buxton. Whereas I, James Barrie, merely feed and clothe and pay all the bills for Michael Llewelyn Davies and, therefore, it seems, have no call upon his affection or his obedience, have been unable to convince him to plan study at Oxford as part of his future through countless months of begging... You, Mr Buxton, have merely to arrive and his future is quite settled.

MARY: James, that's unfair.

BUXTON: I'm sorry if I have unwittingly caused distress, Mr Barrie.

BARRIE: I just felt, Michael, that I might have been the first to have been told of your decision. I am mightily disappointed. Mightily.

MICHAEL: I thought you'd be glad.

BARRIE: Oh, indeed? I feel privileged to have been told at all.

Barrie walks away. Mary goes after him.

MARY: James, wait up. This is not the way.

NICO: I don't understand, Michael. Why is Uncle Jim so angry? I thought he wanted you to go to Oxford?

MICHAEL: So he does, Nico, but he wanted to be the one to convince me of it. I've been so silly. I've hurt his feelings.

SENHOUSE: They can be healed, Davies. A little time. A little patience. And showing him a great deal more attention.

BUXTON: Your Uncle Jim is trying to keep you frozen in time, just like a stopped clock.

BASSETT: Well, that's made a right mess of the picnic. I suppose we all might as well go back to house.

They begin packing away the picnic implements before moving off. Buxton and Bassett are at a distance from the others.

You know I don't like you, Buxton. Not one little bit. But I'm glad you persuaded Davies to go to Oxford.

BUXTON: That's very sporting of you, Bassett. Michael has told me you have more depth than you allow most people to see.

BASSETT: I'm afraid of you, Buxton. Not for myself. For Davies. I don't like what you've done to him.

BUXTON: You've been a good friend to Michael, Bassett. And I hope you continue in that role.

BASSETT: There can be little in the way of friendship between Davies and myself while you're around.

Bassett leaves as Michael approaches.

MICHAEL: What were you and Bassett talking about?

BUXTON: He was just wishing me luck in my endeavour.

MICHAEL: I don't believe you. Bassett would never wish you luck in anything. Why do you lie to me?

BUXTON: To annoy you.

MICHAEL: You know, when you annoy me, I believe I like it. Why is that, Rupert Buxton?

BUXTON: Because, Michael Llewelyn Davies, you like me.

MICHAEL: Can a man really like someone against his will?

BUXTON: Of course he can. That is the nicest way of being liked.

Michael and Buxton exit with the last of the picnic gear.

Scene 4

James Barrie addresses the audience.

BARRIE: At what age are sons the nicest? I do believe Michael was nicest when he was two and knew his alphabet up to G but fell over at H. Or, perhaps, he was best when he was half-past three or just before he struck six, or when he was ill in bed and I asked him in the early morning how he was and he said sternly, 'I don't know, I haven't tried yet.' But, if I can't tell exactly when sons are at their nicest I can certainly ascertain when they are at their most cruel. Oh, Michael, all I've ever wanted for you is that you do everything exquisitely. I do wish in your rush to grow up you could leave me just a few things to do for you still. I suppose it's owing to my having had to be father and mother both to you. And I knew nothing about the bringing up of children. Have I really botched the job so badly that you despise me so? I suspect it is to be my invidious task to watch you grow up from the non-members stand.

Scene 5

The sound of rain pelting against the house. Everyone is bored and restless. Nico is playing music on the Victrola and attempting to get the others to dance. Only Mary seems to be joining in the fun. Barrie is attempting to work on his manuscript. Buxton is posing for Michael.

BARRIE: For heaven's sake turn off that awful noise, I'm trying to concentrate.

NICO: It's the latest music from America, Uncle Jim.

BARRIE: I don't care where it comes from it sounds like a lot of caterwauling. Now turn it off!

MARY: Oh, James, do put away those old papers and come and relax. It will do you good.

BARRIE: I have work to catch up on.

MARY: It's your holiday, James, as much as theirs. It's your last chance to catch up with Michael and Nico before they return to school.

BARRIE: All they want me around for is to pay the bills.

MARY: Whatever is the matter with you, James?

BARRIE: I feel old and unwanted. I feel like twelfth man on my own cricket team.

MARY: Stuff and nonsense. You're just liverish.

BARRIE: Don't patronise me, Mary. The boys have done enough of that already. They talk amongst themselves while I am expected to be a mere ladler out of food.

MARY: You brood too much. Come and join the fun.

BARRIE: You call that awful racket of Nico's fun?

MARY: Michael needs a new model for his sketches. He has done us all till he can do it blindfolded.

BARRIE: I don't wish to encourage his scribbling. He is much too serious about it already.

MARY: Come on. And do try to be cheerful.

Mary drags Barrie into the living area where Michael is sketching Buxton. Senhouse and Nico are practising dance steps and Bassett is peering gloomily at the rain outside.

BASSETT: Nothing is so delightful in Scotland as the leaving of it. Damned rain.

BARRIE: I have shaken my fist at the weather through the window for being so heartless, Mr Bassett. That aside, there's little more I can do.

MICHAEL: Please do be still for a minute, Buxton. You'll ruin my work.

BUXTON: Can't you find another model, Davies? I've a confounded cramp posing for you all evening.

NICO: Do let Buxton up, Michael, he's such a terrific dancer.

MICHAEL: Very well. If you can't take any of this seriously, Buxton, I shall draw still lifes.

BASSETT: You can't get much stiller than the life that's going on around here.

NICO: Please, Uncle Jim, let me turn the music on. It will drown out the rain.

BARRIE: Why is it the young always think the louder a thing is the better? *(sighs)* Go ahead. If you must.

NICO: Thank you, Uncle Jim.

Nico turns on the music and he and Senhouse practise the steps together.

BUXTON: Miss Ansell, would you do me the honour?

MARY: Delighted, Mr Buxton.

Mary and Buxton dance superbly together. Buxton has charm to spare. Nico and Senhouse are openly admiring, Bassett is contemptuous, Michael is jealous and Barrie is hurt. Michael decides it is time to build bridges.

MICHAEL: Why don't you sit for me, Uncle Jim? Let me sketch you.

Barrie examines Michael's sketches.

BARRIE: Are these of Mr Buxton? Why, they are very good.

BUXTON: You sound surprised. Have you never looked at his sketches before?

BARRIE: I have no eye for drawing.

MICHAEL: You were always so adamant about my not being an artist, I thought...

BARRIE: You know that if that is what you really wanted I would not stand in your way.

MICHAEL: You wouldn't help either.

BARRIE: Do you want to sketch me now?

MICHAEL: To me drawing is a form of making love to the subject.

BASSETT: Is that why there are so many pictures of Buxton?

MARY: Mr Bassett, would you care to dance with me? I think I've quite exhausted Rupert.

BASSETT: No thank you all the same. I'd rather be left to my gloom.

Michael begins to sketch Barrie.

BARRIE: Is there a living to be made from portraiture such as this?

NICO: Heaps, Uncle Jim. All the chaps at Eton wanted Michael to draw them.

SENHOUSE: All sorts of people were lining up to be immortalised in crayon or charcoal.

BASSETT: The streets are full of the most uninteresting people so why should we also be subjected to them on the walls of our art galleries?

BARRIE: Why indeed, Mr Bassett?

BASSETT: Why should our walls be covered with portraits of old men? Why not young men? Young women? People in their prime rather than their dotage.

BARRIE: I hardly think of myself as in my dotage although some people would have me dead and buried given half a chance.

BASSETT: There should be a ban on portraits of anyone over the age of 30. Particularly if they are bald.

MICHAEL: Bassett!

BUXTON: Steady on, Bassett. You forget yourself.

BARRIE: Always ready to jump to my defence, Mr Buxton. Quite admirable but I am able to fend for myself. And what do you suggest I do for my baldness, Mr Bassett?

BASSETT: That remark was not aimed at you in particular, Mr Barrie. But since you ask, I have the address of an excellent hair restorer.

BARRIE: I can just see myself setting forth. Choosing a day, much like this one, when I can dodge in under the concealment of an umbrella. You don't seem to be aware, Mr Bassett, that I am rather fond of my bald spot. We have become good friends through centuries of shared adventures. Sometimes, though, I do wish I could cut myself this way *(indicates cutting off some of his bulk)* and elongate myself that way *(indicates he would like to be taller)* and remove the crows-feet and bring back the smile and generally drop half a century. That I would do with much joyful perturbation.

His speech brings on a coughing fit during which Michael hides his sketches of Barrie and puts away his artist's materials.

BASSETT: For heaven's sake, I can't stand that blasted coughing a moment longer.

MARY: James, I think that cough has gone to your chest.

BARRIE: It's odd, Mr Bassett. I'm quite taken aback when people say 'What a cough you have'. I suppose it's a little like Big Ben, though perhaps not quite as loud, but so frequent that I have ceased to notice it. If it bothers you, however, I will take it away.

MARY: Have you brought your medicine?

Barrie nods.

BARRIE: If you would be good enough to administer the dose.

MICHAEL: Uncle Jim? Can't you do without it for now?

MARY: None of us will get any rest tonight if James can't sleep.

BASSETT: I couldn't stand another night of that hacking.

BARRIE: It's getting late. I bid you gentlemen au revoir for this evening.

NICO: Good night, Uncle Jim.

MICHAEL: Bon soir, Uncle Jim. Pleasant dreams.

Mary helps Barrie out. She puts him to bed and administers the injection while the good night scene continues simultaneously.

BASSETT: I suppose I shall turn in, too. Sleep is preferable to this tedium.

Exits.

SENHOUSE: Probably not such a bad idea, Bassett.

Glancing conspiratorially at Michael and Buxton.

Coming Nico?

NICO: I thought I might stay and listen to a few more records. And talk to Michael and Buxton. They know so many super things.

SENHOUSE: Then I shall just have to look through the latest magazines from America on my own.

NICO: You have magazines from America, Senhouse?

SENHOUSE: A few. And they have pictures of the latest fashions that all the chaps are wearing.

NICO: I say, could I have a look?

SENHOUSE: You'll know what to wear next season before anyone else.

NICO: Do you mind awfully Michael? Buxton?

MICHAEL: Go ahead, Nico.

BUXTON: Go to it, Nico.

NICO: *(racing out)* Come on, Senhouse. Don't be all night about it.

SENHOUSE: Goodnight Davies. Buxton.

MICHAEL: Senhouse.

BUXTON: And thanks.

Senhouse exits.

I thought they would never go.

Michael and Buxton settle in front of the fire.

MICHAEL: I suppose we should go to bed, too.

BUXTON: Stay... at least until the fire goes out.

MICHAEL: Perhaps I should stoke it.

BUXTON: If you really think it needs it.

Michael makes no effort to move.

MICHAEL: It is getting terribly late. We should follow the example of the others.

BUXTON: All joy departed Paris when you left in such a hurry. It was as if you had packed it up and taken it away in your suitcase.

MICHAEL: I'm surprised you even noticed I'd gone.

BUXTON: If you'd known how much you were missed you would have been very pleased indeed. The lift at the pensione even got sulky and took to creaking at me as if your leaving was my fault. It was most forlorn.

MICHAEL: It was your fault. As well you know.

BUXTON: The fire kept going out. I sometimes thought of following its example and seeking company in a cafe but the desperate idea came to nothing. As an alternative I had the concierge bring me two teacups every hour.

MICHAEL: What? Only two cups of tea?

BUXTON: When I did venture forth to have a little dinner with myself I found we did not get on so very well together.

MICHAEL: All right. You're forgiven. Though I suspect you've been practising your pretty speeches for days.

BUXTON: I do believe if you were left alone with a carrot you would be radiant to it so as not to hurt its feelings.

MICHAEL: All right then. You were a swine in Paris. Is that better? Why did you do it?

BUXTON: To impress you. I wanted to be friends.

MICHAEL: It almost prevented our friendship.

BUXTON: I wouldn't have let it.

MICHAEL: You might not have had a choice.

BUXTON: Yes I would. You see, Michael, I dare to go further than most. At Harrow I had a special friend. My family, a particularly old-fashioned lot, didn't like it and tried to keep us apart. We ran away to Newcastle.

MICHAEL: To where?

BUXTON: We had an idyllic week together.

MICHAEL: Where is he now?

BUXTON: *(shrugs)* Father was waiting at the station on my return. He thrashed me with his riding crop.

MICHAEL: Poor Rupert.

BUXTON: I was locked away like poor mad Bertha in *Jane Eyre*. Luckily the doctor was a sympathetic chap from Zurich and when I was caught flirting with the nurses he proclaimed me cured.

MICHAEL: And are you?

BUXTON: I swear to God I'll never betray your love.

MICHAEL: I thought you said you were an atheist.

BUXTON: How do you answer?

They move to each other and kiss. Barrie in his bedroom suddenly sits bolt upright. He is disorientated under the influence of heroin.

BARRIE: Where is it? Where is it? It must be here somewhere. What is it he does not want me to see? Am I portrayed as a monster? The very devil himself? A possessive dragon preying on the young and innocent?

He slips in and out of delusions believing momentarily he is Captain Hook.

How still the night is; nothing sounds alive. Now is the hour when children in their homes are a-bed; their lips bright-browned with the goodnight chocolate, and their tongues drowsily searching for belated crumbs housed insecurely on their shining cheeks. Compare with them the children on this boat about to walk the plank. Split my infinitives, but tis the hour of my triumph. And yet some disky spirit compels me now to make my dying speech, lest when dying there may be no time for it. All mortals envy me, yet better perhaps for Hook to have had less ambition! Oh fame, fame, thou glittering bauble, *(what if the very ...)*

Nico enters.

NICO: Uncle Jim! Uncle Jim!

BARRIE: You, boy, you look as if you had a little pluck in you. Didst never want to be a pirate?

Mary and Michael enter.

MARY: Come away, Nico.

NICO: What's wrong with Uncle Jim, Michael?

MICHAEL: It's nothing, Nico. Go back to bed. It's just the medicine for his bronchitis sometimes makes him a little... unsettled.

BARRIE: Where has he hidden the treasure? I must find it! I must.

He begins searching his bed. Senhouse enters.

SENHOUSE: What's going on here?

BARRIE: Do you boys want a touch of the cat before you walk the plank? Fetch the cat-o'-nine-tails.

MARY: Take Nico out of this, Mr Senhouse. Keep him occupied while we look after James.

NICO: He will be all right, won't he? Uncle Jim, I mean?

SENHOUSE: It's just the strain from writing his new play.

Nico and Senhouse exit. Barrie finds the pictures of him that Michael has drawn.

BARRIE: Oh, wretched boy, is that how you see me? What a diabolical aptitude for finding my worst attributes. I indignantly deny them!

He crumples up the pictures and casts them aside.

If I believed they did me justice I would throw myself from the highest peak.

MICHAEL: Uncle Jim, I didn't mean...

MARY: Shh.

BARRIE: The ship's bewitched. Never was luck on a pirate ship wi' a woman aboard. Throw the girl overboard. Cleave her to the brisket!

Barrie has found his walking stick and is lunging wildly at Mary as Buxton enters.

So, Peter Pan, this is all your doing?

Buxton sizes up the situation and assumes the role of Peter Pan.

BUXTON: Aye, James Hook, it is all my doing.

BARRIE: Proud and insolent youth, prepare to meet thy doom.

BUXTON: Dark and sinister man, I take on thy challenge.

Barrie swings his cane wildly just missing Buxton.

BARRIE: Tis some fiend fighting me! Pan, who and what art thou?

BUXTON: I'm youth, I'm joy, I'm a little bird that has broken out of the egg!

Barrie reaches out to touch Buxton but collapses before he can do so. Mary covers Barrie with a blanket.

MARY: He'll remember none of this in the morning.

Buxton and Michael leave together, Buxton with his arm across Michael's shoulders in comfort. Mary lingers and makes sure Barrie is comfortable. When she has finished she addresses the audience.

MARY: James Barrie was a generous man but not a loving one. At least not to me. He was also a clever man and it was my destiny to love only clever men. James and my second husband, Gilbert Cannan. The reason I love my dogs so passionately is that they can never be ungenerous as men are ungenerous. They could never be complicated as men are complicated. Perhaps my love for dogs in the beginning was a sort of mother love for I had no children by James. He preferred other people's children. And, too, I was an adult, and he is not very good with adults. Except, perhaps, mothers. And I was never a mother. But he bestowed his charity on me. He gave me sufficient to live out my life in comfort. He meant it kindly but I always felt smothered by it. Even though I returned to Paris and remained a continent away from him, I felt the tentacles of his smothering pity until the day he died. Alas those who did not have the safety net of distance between themselves and James.

Scene 6

Barrie and Michael are strolling near Sandford-on-Thames, just south of Oxford.

BARRIE: Are you happy here, Michael?

MICHAEL: It was awfully hard to adjust at first, but Buxton has been a tower of strength. He's very popular. Senhouse is mixing with the Bloomsbury set. They seem quite taken with him and he's meeting everyone there is to know on the literary scene. Bassett, in his usual fashion, doesn't approve, of course. He thinks the Bloomsbury's too avant garde. And he doesn't approve of the subject matter on which some modern novelists write. He maintains that some subjects should be left to doctors. It has a lot to do with the fact his parents have decided on a career in politics for him and he has become conscious, some would say self-conscious, of virtue. Bassett feels it incumbent upon himself to interfere in everyone else's life.

BARRIE: Tell Mr Bassett from me that the novelist's canvas is all humanity and that there is no part of it which he has not the right to treat. By his subject never, by his treatment always, should he be judged. I don't know how it is with you, Michael, or with young Buxton, but when I meet a man who is constantly quoting proverbs about the virtue of a bird in the hand over its brothers in the bush, I may continue to respect him but I keep him at arm's length. From that time on he's no longer an intimate of mine. Mr Bassett sounds as if he has already assumed the attributes of a politician.

MICHAEL: I am glad I came to Oxford.

BARRIE: It's everything I ever dreamed for you.

MICHAEL: You don't have to dream for me, Uncle Jim. I have my own now.

NICO: I say, Michael, what a splendid lake. What is it called?

MICHAEL: Sandford Pool. It's one of my favourite spots.

BARRIE: It's a great spot for rowing. Right, Mr Buxton?

BUXTON: Indeed. Or to relax or swat before examinations.

NICO: What's the big obelisk for, Uncle Jim?

BARRIE: That commemorates two great friends who drowned together in the pool in 1843.

NICO: How terribly sad.

BARRIE: One young man got into difficulties while bathing and his friend swam out to rescue him but both, unfortunately, lost their lives. The water is very treacherous.

MICHAEL: What an odd expression, 'to lose one's life'. As if one has merely misplaced it and it will turn up again somewhere if one goes looking for it.

NICO: And do their ghosts haunt the shores? Are their spirits guardians of this very place?

BUXTON: Their spirits live atop the obelisk, Nico, and whenever true friends come down here they gaze at the living and weep. For they know that friendships, no matter how strong, will one day end. Theirs, though, is for all eternity.

BARRIE: The true test of friendship is its tenacity. But genuine affection between two men, innocent affection, is like a grenade in the midst of society. People find it effeminate.

But there is no greater love than that between two friends unless it is that of a father for his son. Did I ever tell you about re-meeting, a few years ago this is now, a friend of my infancy and I was delighted to discover I was as attached to him as ever. He's an ironmonger now and my oldest recollection is his running to my house - we were about five - to tell me an old man we knew had cut his throat with a razor and if I came quick I should see the blood. And I did.

NICO: Come on, Uncle Jim. I can see a boat.

BARRIE: Rowing a boat at my age.

Barrie and Nico exit.

BUXTON: Is anything the matter?

MICHAEL: It was the thought of those poor drowned friends.

BUXTON: Shall we meet again, dear friend,

> When the Winter's at an end,
>
> And Spring goes dancing down the woodland ways:
>
> When the old grey tired earth
>
> Wakens at her sunny mirth
>
> And smiles to think of Golden Summer days?
>
> Shall we meet again, dear friend,
>
> When the blossomed branches bend

And woo the earth with perfumed sighs, and
weep

Their beautiful starry tears;

When the last red sunbeam peers

At the first red rose of summer in her sleep?

Shall we meet again, dear friend,

When the leaves of Autumn blend

Their fiery tints with evening skies of gold,

When the dews are on the grass,

And the west winds softly pass

And breathe no whisper of the Winter's cold?

We shall meet again, I'm sure,

For the Gifts of God endure

Eternally, beyond the reach of pain;

And, if you should die, I know,

Ere the light of hope burns low,

Your spirit will come back to me again.

Scene 7

Senhouse addresses the audience.

SENHOUSE: Michael and Buxton became inseparable. Some
people said to an unhealthy degree. For all their other-
worldliness, Michael and Buxton, were both fine exponents

of that supreme expression of the Edwardian era - cricket, and played remarkably by the rules. But for my taste the world was changing and rules were meant only for the bending or breaking. Our paths crossed frequently although I had been supplanted in Michael's affections. I had found new avenues and I threw myself enthusiastically into their exploration while they embarked on a walking expedition of the South Downs. Michael wrote to me of the beauty of the country, the joy of the flowers and the scents of life to which his friend Buxton was introducing him although it was difficult to discern whether it was the charm of the countryside or the charm of Rupert Buxton which most bedazzled him.

> *Michael and Buxton are arm in arm on their walking tour when Buxton gives Michael a flower. Michael pulls the petals off in a parody of "he loves me, he loves me not" and shrugs in resignation at the end.*

MICHAEL: Can there be a more exquisite way to spend one's holidays? *(pause)* I do love you.

BUXTON: Did you need the petals of that poor dismembered flower to prove it to yourself?

MICHAEL: Damn it, you're supposed to say that you love me too. It's the convention.

BUXTON: If it's convention you're after, then don't love me. You don't need me to tell you like one of those flowery greeting cards. You do realise, don't you, that he loves you the way I do?

MICHAEL: Buxton!

BUXTON: It's true. I've watched him.

MICHAEL: He loves me and my brothers.

BUXTON: Yes, but you're the special one, the one he's in love with.

MICHAEL: He's never touched me and he never would.

BUXTON: That's his tragedy.

MICHAEL: I can't see Uncle Jim as a tragic figure.

BUXTON: Still, I make love enough to you for both of us.

MICHAEL: Shh! Someone might hear you.

BUXTON: Always afraid of being overheard.

MICHAEL: It's not that I don't want to shout it. But Uncle Jim...

BUXTON: He wouldn't approve?

MICHAEL: No!

BUXTON: I think not

MICHAEL: Will it really be so terrible?

BUXTON: Unless we move to France or Italy.

MICHAEL: That seems like running away somehow.

BUXTON: I thought you wanted to live in Paris.

MICHAEL: I would have been able to come home. Are you sure this is what you want?

BUXTON: Why do you doubt it?

MICHAEL: Because you could pass. You could marry and have children.

BUXTON: So could you, Michael.

MICHAEL: No. I'm not like you. I can't turn my emotions in either direction. I'm like Senhouse in that regard. Shall you make me very unhappy?

BUXTON: Not intentionally.

Scene 8

Barrie addresses the audience.

BARRIE: I remember one of the last occasions on which I saw Michael. He and Nico had come into town to see me and to make a day of sorting out old furniture before it was sold and disposed of. It was what they had grown up with. Hundreds of familiar articles once very pretty and much cared for, now dusty, disregarded and clammy cold in the storage place. There were even garments of the days when they were babes. Many things they once exulted in. But they had grown older. Children no longer and there was no sentiment about the visit, only a bored look at the dead. There is nothing to complain of in this, it's how the young must take tomorrow on their shoulders. But I felt as if I were one of the articles lying there much more than one of the onlookers. I felt like one of the items from their past for which they now had no use.

Scene 9

Oxford. Senhouse is reading aloud from toward the end of a manuscript of E.M. Forster's novel Maurice while Michael rests his head in Buxton's lap.

BUXTON: Bravo, Maurice. Michael, whatever is the matter?

MICHAEL: That's the most beautiful thing I've ever heard.

SENHOUSE: He doesn't kill himself in the end. He and Alec run away together and live happily ever after it seems.

BUXTON: When will Mr Forster publish?

SENHOUSE: He won't. It's doing the rounds of those sympathetic members of literary circles in manuscript form. They all like it but recommend against publishing. They fear he'll be prosecuted for obscenity. The statutes are harsh.

BUXTON: It would also expose Mr Forster.

SENHOUSE: His mother is still alive.

MICHAEL: Doesn't he see the importance for us? It has a happy ending. No one commits suicide. No one dies as they usually do in such books.

SENHOUSE: All the more reason for the authorities to find it obscene. The characters accept themselves for what they are. No socially redeeming death. They'd accuse the novel of proselytising.

BUXTON: Mr Forster's a brave man for having written it. It could easily fall into the wrong hands.

MICHAEL: It offers so much hope.

BUXTON: So why be unhappy?

MICHAEL: I wonder had there been a book like this available would those two poor friends have drowned themselves at Sandford Pool?

BUXTON: Would you like to walk down there and make peace with them?

MICHAEL: Shall we?

BUXTON: Coming with us, Senhouse?

SENHOUSE: I have to return this manuscript. They're afraid of having it out of their hands for too long.

Bassett comes in slightly drunk.

MICHAEL: Bassett! What are you doing here?

BASSETT: Come to visit my once-upon-a-time friends.

Senhouse gets ready to leave.

Going so soon, Senhouse? Isn't my company to your liking?

SENHOUSE: Quite frankly, Bassett, it's not. Not until you tone down that holier-than-thou attitude you've developed.

BASSETT: Your way of life is wholly deplorable. It reeks of corruption and vice. You three are offensive to every decent man and woman in England.

MICHAEL: I thought you were our friend.

BASSETT: I'm no friend to unnatural acts. Or scandal.

MICHAEL: Since when is love a scandal?

BASSETT: Your sort of love has always been a scandal.

BUXTON: Just why is that, Bassett?

BASSETT: Because, Buxton, it's against the natural order of things.

BUXTON: That's odd! My heart did not come with a book of instructions. If yours did, Bassett, perhaps you'd be good enough to lend it to me.

BASSETT: There's no future for you, you know that, don't you? There can only be disgrace. Or imprisonment.

BUXTON: Always the optimist, Bassett.

BASSETT: I blame you for all this, Buxton. Davies, Senhouse and I had the perfect friendship until you came along and destroyed it with your perverted behaviour.

SENHOUSE: Look, Bassett, what's got into you?

BASSETT: My God, you haven't heard, have you?

MICHAEL: Heard what, Bassett?

BASSETT: About Edward Marjoribanks.

SENHOUSE: What about him?

BASSETT: They caught him. In Kensington Gardens.

MICHAEL: Oh, my God!

BASSETT: It's in all the newspapers.

SENHOUSE: I must go to him at once.

BASSETT: No. No. No. Senhouse, you really don't understand.

BUXTON: What don't we understand, Bassett?

BASSETT: That happened days ago. But with his family connections, well, they managed to keep it out of the newspapers at the time. The old boys network, that sort of thing. Favours swapped at the top.

MICHAEL: So how did they find out?

BASSETT: He couldn't stand the shame, you see. The humiliation. Didn't want to implicate his friends. I underestimated him. A real gentleman was Marjoribanks. Used his father's pistol. Blew his brains out like he knew he had to. It was the only way. Can you understand now why I've been so hard on you? I don't want you to end up like Marjoribanks.

BUXTON: We're not so foolish as to do things in Kensington Gardens.

BASSETT: But you do at Sandford Pool. At night.

MICHAEL: That's our own private business.

BASSETT: So private the Dean knows all about it.

MICHAEL: What?

BUXTON: How?

BASSETT: You've never been discreet, either of you. The whole of Oxford knows about you. The Dean is in the process of writing a letter to your Uncle Jim, Davies, and to your parents, Buxton. A letter explaining the serious implications of your friendship. And also warning that you'll both end up like Marjoribanks. He intends to send you down if the relationship between the two of you is not severed immediately.

MICHAEL: Buxton?

BUXTON: We'll fight it!

BASSETT: You can't win. The game has always been more important than the individuals who make up the team.

SENHOUSE: Poor Marjoribanks.

Scene 10

Barrie addresses the audience.

BARRIE: Love is such a messy emotion. And, when all is said and done, love is an emotion not a physical act. It makes monsters of those caught in its thrall. They can be as hard as nails, as cruel as the grave, as cynical as the fiend, and as warm, trusting, tender and painfully sensitive as feathers in an eider down. It's a brave man who allows himself to feel love. It's a warrior who abandons himself to its all-pervasive warmth for no man comes away from the experience unscathed. It's the wise man who turns his back on love and learns to live without it.

Scene 11

Moonlight. Michael and Buxton at Sandford Pool.

MICHAEL: Do you think they're watching us now?

BUXTON: Especially now.

MICHAEL: Do you think spirits can be happy?

BUXTON: Wouldn't you be happy if we could be together for always? For eternity?

MICHAEL: If only we could talk to them. To see how they felt. To see if they would change it all if they could.

BUXTON: To die would be an awfully big adventure.

MICHAEL: Uncle Jim will be completely devastated. There'll be a big scandal. Perhaps even ruin his career. Peter Pan is a pervert. The newspapers will have a field day.

BUXTON: We could always run away to Europe.

MICHAEL: Fleeing to Europe won't help Uncle Jim. Or Nico. Or my other brothers.

BUXTON: Michael, this is your life, your happiness we're talking about.

MICHAEL: No, it's not just my life. I have others to consider.

BUXTON: If they truly love you, all they will care about is your happiness.

MICHAEL: If growing up means becoming like all the rest, I hope I never grow up.

BUXTON: Do you regret our meeting, Michael?

MICHAEL: Of course not.

BUXTON: Then what's the answer?

MICHAEL: Obviously it is still too soon for happy endings.

Michael begins to remove his clothing and Buxton follows suit slowly. They remove their shoes and socks and their outer garments helping each other from time to time. They move to the water, then suddenly and violently they fling their arms around each other and slide to their knees. They remain in that position for the remainder of the play.

BARRIE: I dreamed that he came back to me and we went on in the old way, till the fatal 19th approached again, and he became very sad. He rose in the night and put on old clothes and came to look at me as he thought, asleep. I tried to prevent his going, but he had to and I knew it. He said he thought it would be harder if I didn't let him go alone. But I went with him, holding his hand, and he liked it, and when we came to the place, he said, 'Goodbye, Uncle Jim.' and went into the pool and sank, just as before. Everything is different to me now. Michael was very much my world. It is as if, long after writing *Peter Pan*, its true meaning has become apparent to me: the desperate, but unsuccessful attempt of a boy to grow up.

He is totally devastated.

BASSETT: *(addressing the audience)* Two men who had witnessed Michael's death testified that the water was as still as a mill-pond at the time. One of them stated that he heard a shout. He looked in the direction and saw two men bathing in the pool in difficulties. Their heads were close together - they were standing in the water and not struggling. He formed the impression that they were clasped.

NICO: *(addressing the audience)* I remember when my brother Peter brought me to Uncle Jim's flat after the news of Michael's death, he cried out, 'Oh, take him away, take him away!' Strangely I was not hurt by this, rather I understood in some way how my very closeness to Michael made his more or less uncontrollable grief even more uncontrollable. My first duty was to go and break the news to Senhouse. I was riding on the top of the bus when I saw him walking along the street. I ran back to him and he immediately knew what had happened by the look on my face. We stood in a doorway and sobbed together.

SENHOUSE: *(addressing the audience)* The two bodies were not recovered until the following afternoon and an inquest held at Oxford a day later. The jury returned a verdict of accidental drowning and expressed the opinion that Buxton lost his life in his endeavour to save his friend. Following the inquest Davies' body was brought back to James Barrie's flat. Barrie looked like a man in a nightmare and had not slept for days. He had to be prescribed heroin to help him sleep and he stayed shut away in his study. During that unimaginable weekend there were moments of terrible danger when Barrie's overwhelming desire was to end a life made utterly pointless without Michael.

BARRIE: Death? It's a sudden idea which comes to us in the middle of our living. Someone who has died is only a little way ahead in a procession in which we are all moving in the same direction. When we round the corner we'll see him again. We have only lost him for a moment because we fell behind, stopping to tie a shoe-lace.

THE END

Lydian Press

Made in the USA
Charleston, SC
02 February 2014